I0390453

# THE EXPERT'S GUIDE
# TO
# CREATING AND
# SELLING
# THE BRAND

# AND
# THE EXPERT'S GUIDE
# TO
# CYBER-SECURITY

BY
WARREN BROWN

GOLDCOPY PUBLICATION
LONDON
2012

THE EXPERT'S GUIDE TO

CREATING AND SELLING THE BRAND

AND

CYBER-SECURITY

ISBN 978-1-291-21638-7

GOLDCOPY PUBLICATIONS

Copyright @Warren Brown.   London. 2012

OTHER BOOKS BY WARREN BROWN
The Secret Race Anglo-Indians
World Recipes for a High Income Business
Discover Parallel Universes
The Anglo-Indian Race Preservation Course
The Lady of the Sea and other Poems

Acknowledgments
To all those who assisted me with the research work
for this book.

# INTRODUCTION

We are all familiar with the brands advertised in the media today. Yet, many of us do not know how to create our own brand to promote our product or service. So this book will help you to discover the essentials necessary for building and creating a profitable brand.

Sincerely
Warren Brown
London
2012


This Book will help you to.....

1. Put together the essentials for your Brand
2. To present your brand in the best possible way
3. To make your brand with your own Unique Selling Proposition.
4. To make a brand which stands above the others.
5. To make your brand visible in the public eye for a long time to come
6. To make your brand a Profit Label, to generate a constant flow of revenue
7. To make your Brand a Status symbol which every consumer in your Niche market wants to own
8. To make everyone want your Brand product and willing to pay for it.
9. To make profit the obvious outcome for your brand, with repeated sales.
10. To make your Brand deliver Consumer satisfaction Guaranteed.

# The Art of Internet Branding

## What is Internet Branding?

Internet branding is one strategy that business owners can employ to establishing their position in the marketplace. Even well-established companies are investing on creating an online brand reputation since internet branding strategies have also produced massive impact on a brand's effort to expand. This is most important these days wherein the internet has taken on a significant role in the everyday lives of the consumers. Hence, you need to utilize it as one of the means that you can communicate your message to them.

With internet branding, you are basically utilizing the tools provided by the internet as a leverage to all your marketing efforts. The objective with using the internet as a medium for promoting your brand works the same way as any other branding methods, which is to increase the demand for the products in your brand.

## Importance of Internet Branding

Every business owner is aware of the benefits that a good brand can make for your company. Since the brand is basically what distinguishes you from any other companies that offer the same product or service, you must execute your branding strategies properly to produce the results you want. Take a look at some successful brands in the industry, who have become so distinct to the point wherein their names have been associated with a certain product. This is what business owners must try to aim for.

In business terms, this is referred to as brand positioning. It establishes the main locus of your product to the target market. Therefore, you will be utilizing the specific features that makes your product distinct from the other and use that as a focus of your message in the internet branding effort. Indeed, product differentiation and product positioning are closely linked to one another. These are two basic ploys that you can utilize in your internet branding strategies to "own" a segment of the market and produce a loyal customer base from that.

Is It Worth Investing In?

Several companies and brands have worked so hard on establishing their brand and yet they fail to look into the possibilities of producing an online brand. Hence, they lose that advantage to other brands who worked on appealing to the consumers and making their offer known.

However, if you opt to embark on an internet branding strategy, you must not also neglect the positive value or message that you are trying to impart with regards to your company. To sum it up, a good internet branding strategy is worth your investment. So, don't just go right into an online campaign for your brand. It must be something that is a product of your thorough evaluation and planning.

## What About Small Businesses?

Despite the large impact of the online industry in people's lives these days, it is only projected to grow in the years to come. Hence, this makes the internet an even more reliable avenue to expand their marketing efforts. The best thing about the internet is that it provides an even playing field for big- and small-time businesses to promote their brand. Even new businesses can utilize the internet as a means to position their brand and make their existence known in the market. So, it's no longer new these days to have new products or brands introduced online as it is one of the fastest growing industries today.

And yet, the benefits of offering your products and brand to a larger market is beneficial for small time businesses since potential buyers can focus only on the quality of service and performance. By maintaining the value and continually differentiating your product, then internet branding will offer several potential benefits for your business.

## The Significance of Logo in Branding Strategy

### Creating Company Logo

In addition to creating a unique name, designing your own distinct logo is another effective branding strategy that every business owner can employ. Aside from the name, having a logo to attach to that image reinforces the potential power that your brand has in the market. As a factor that compels customers to pick your brand out of other competing businesses, this is something that every businessman need not take lightly.

Visual recognition is the main purpose of a business or brand logo. Therefore, you need to produce a logo design that would easily stand out and be recognized. There are two steps involved in the process of creating a logo: first is conceptualization and then execution.

The conceptualization part is where you extract ideas from the message that you want your brand to convey to the consumers. Then, the execution part is where you produce creative ideas that will make tangible that concept you have for your brand. The execution part is the most vital part in this process because a good concept could still fail if not executed properly. Here is also where you should decide on the color or styles used in the logo.

Significance of a Logo

Logos are an integral part of a company's branding strategy mainly because it is a visual representation of the company. For instance, companies create simple yet elegant designs to produce the idea of stability and trust. Meanwhile, other companies create an interactive and complex design to showcase the different features of the company.

Going back to the creation process of a logo, the information that you want to reveal about the company and its product will serve as basis for the creation of the concept for your logo. The same goes with how you utilize the design to showcase those information. There are different methods done to achieve this but you can perform some brainstorming to get the ideas out.

Logo as a Branding Strategy

The company is logo is the most important part in the creation of company image. It can be used as a trademark for the company to represent its existence and identity in the market. As compared to most advertising campaigns, a successful logo is one that is able to stay in the memory of the customers at a longer time and be able to appeal to their attention. This is crucial whenever you have several other similar businesses trying to achieve the same.

If you have decided on a final design for your company logo, then you can utilize that on various mediums such as websites, billiards, ad spaces, business cards, promotional items, and many more. If you did a successful job on the creation alone, the presence of the logo itself will serve as a reminder to people about your company and what type of business you do.

Protecting Your Logo

Since the logo is now a representation or visual image of your company, you must do your best to safeguard it and protect your company's reputation in the market. If possible, you must patent your logo once you have decided on using it. Since you have invested much on it, you have to ensure that it is solely the property of your company. This applies not just for large-scale companies, but even for small ones as well.

Also, when you are working with somebody else in designing the logo, such as a logo design firm, opt only for those legitimate ones. This would help possible cases of infringement or to protect the reputation of your own company. After all, the main essence behind creating a logo as a branding strategy is to create your business identity.

What is Brand Equity?

Brand Equity Defined

Brand equity is a marketing term used to refer to the marketing impact of a given product in association with a brand name. It tries to examine how a given product will perform in the market if it did not have the privilege of that brand name. Therefore, the basis for brand equity and its impact on a business is based on the knowledge of the customer about that product. And yet, brand plays a vital role in helping build that knowledge and awareness, as well as the choices they make based on that knowledge.

Brand equity, then, reinforces the significance of a brand's value and produce that positive type of recall in the mind of consumers. Marketing research has revealed that brand equity is one of the most important asset to the company.

Three Perspectives of Brand Equity

As an intangible asset, brand equity only gets its meaning out of the perceived quality and associations made by a consumer on a given product. Brand equity can be viewed in three different perspectives:

• Financial: One way to understand the value of brand equity is to calculate the premium that is placed on a product. To further understand, take for example two types of products: one that is of a recognized brand, and the other is unrecognized brand. Consumers are willing to pay a bigger amount for the branded product over those which they are unfamiliar with.

• Brand Extensions: When certain products attain a certain level of commercial success, most companies consider extending their line by introducing newer products under their brand. Because of the existing brand awareness, these companies will no longer invest on large advertising expenditures just to make that newly introduced product known.

• Consumer-based: The trust and attitude exhibited by a customer towards a given product is impacted by the associations they make with that brand. Oftentimes, these associations are a product of their own experience with using the brand. Therefore, actual experience plays a crucial role in the marketing strategy, especially in a developing brand.

Benefits of a Strong Brand Equity

Not all brand equity is positive, therefore most companies invest on building a strong brand equity. After all, it offers several benefits to the company. Below are just some of the helpful benefits that a company can derive of a good brand equity:

• Establishes a more reliable stream of income.

• By increasing brand equity, companies are also able to increase their profits through increased market share and premium pricing for less promotional costs.

• If you have established a good brand, then you can sell that brand name at a given price.

Managing Brand Equity

There are three stages involved in creating, building, and managing your company's brand equity. They are outlined below:

1.) Your first step involves the introduction of a product of a given brand into the market. You must establish a certain standard for that brand to be able to launch products in the future that will sell in the market. Your aim here is to produce a positive response from the consumer to build trust among consumers.

2.) Try to produce a brand that is unique and yet memorable. The attitude of your brand must be accessible to consumers and must also provide benefits to satisfy its users.

3.) Consistency is the key. Your message must be synchronized with your company's overall image and reinforce the value espoused by your organization. This is one of the most effective ways to build a strong brand equity.

**Basic Models Used For Branding Plan**

Branding is a product of intense planning and conceptualization. To come up with innovative marketing ideas and an effective way to brand your products, you need to carefully lay out the steps you need to get there. Doing so will also enable you to take note of the vital aspects involved in the creation of a brand. Brand models have been formulated to create the framework needed to build an effective brand that will be able to withstand market trends and competition.

What is a Branding Model?

There are basic models utilized in the process of brand planning. Each of them will cover different scopes and aspects of the process to create a sound branding strategy. Aside from the ability to postulate methods for arriving at a specific brand idea, these models will also help businessmen understand the behavior of consumers in terms of their responses to a brand, which is helpful in adjusting old branding strategies or acquiring new ones.

All of these features are key in managing and reviewing brands, which are necessary steps that must be taken by any company in their branding efforts. These models are not directly linked but one does impact another.

Brand Positioning

This model involves your effort to create an image that will have its distinct position in the market. Firmly establishing your brand will help your target market to easily remember and and opt for your line of products. This is one aspect of your brand planning wherein you must focus on creating superior brands that will eliminate your competition. Here are steps you need to look into:

*This is the step wherein you begin to identify other brands you are competing against. Then, define the parameters of your own brand against your competition. This will enable you to focus your efforts.

*Next, your objective is to introduce attributes to your brand that will enable it to stand out from competition. You must also introduce elements into your brand that will produce in the mind of your consumers or target market the perceived quality of your brand.

*You must establish a slogan for your brand that will aim to reaffirm the position and values of your brand. It aims to articulate the message of the brand and what it promises to deliver to the consumers.

Brand Resonance

Once you're through the stage of creation and distinction placement in the market, your next step is to protect the loyalty of your consumers. To do that, you need to employ an efficient customer relation service and to provide a feedback system. This model follows from the initial steps laid out by the brand positioning methods. Now that have acquired target customers, your next aim is to strengthen the relationship between them and your brand. After all, majority of the business sales stem from repeat customers.

More than anything, this stage is where you must reinforce the messages initially conveyed by your brand. Hence, customers will remain satisfied with the level of performance and quality delivered by your brand. Are your methods consistent to the identity of the brand and its missions? Take into consideration the feedback of customers on your product and how you can build up on that relationship.

Brand Value Chain

This one is more focused on the financial impact of your branding efforts. The basic idea of this model is that the value of the brand consist in the customers, so that is where you should be focusing most of your branding strategies on.

Carefully combining these various models will provide a company a reliable perspective of the different areas involved in the marketing activity. Taking bringing all these branding steps into the formula will enable you to easily track progress or problem areas in the branding system.

Boost Your Branding With A Slogan

What is a Slogan?

Any form of business branding plan must involve the creation of a slogan. It is one of the basic elements necessary in building an effective brand campaign. A slogan typically consists of a short sentence or a phrase that serve to reinforce the business name or logo. In fact, many big time businesses has created highly successful marketing slogans that it has been recognized by the consumers as much as their name.

Slogan is often dismissed as an element for effective branding methods, which is also the reason why even a potentially good business name fails to deliver. Its purpose main purpose is mainly to enhance and boost the name or provide a tiny glimpse of what the brand promises to deliver. Even simple words or phrases can go a long way when it works well with your brand.

Impact of Slogan to Branding

Brand recall is the main purpose of creating a slogan. They are there to speak for the brand where images fail. This further enables the brand to create a more lasting memory to the minds of the consumers and enhances the market reach of the product.

Therefore, you need not just produce a creative slogan but an intelligent one. The purpose is mainly to capture the consumer's attention and produce interest about a given product. It enables your audience to stop and think about the possibilities offered by the brand. Depending on your marketing plan, you can utilize a slogan to appeal to either the needs, attitudes, or emotions of the consumers. Therefore, you are trying to compel them to make an action, which in this case is to purchase the product to avail of the benefits it offer.

Why is it such a potent part of your marketing and branding efforts, you may ask? Because it triggers the motivation of the consumers then driving them into action.

Creating a Good Slogan

Due to the importance of the slogan in your business, it is best to assert careful planning into the process of creating a slogan. To achieve a good slogan, you must inform yourself of what the qualities of a good slogan are.

1.) A good slogan is memorable. Since the purpose of a slogan is to increase brand recall and trigger buyer motivations, it must first be able to capture their attention and stay in their memory for a given period. Staying power is an essential factor in the business industry, so you have to be able to produce something that stays in the mind of the consumers when they go out to buy.

2.) A good slogan produces images on the consumer's mind. Most people produce images on their mind when they hear something. Hence, you can trigger the visual patterns of your customers by using the slogan. For instance, you can remind them about your company logo and create a stronger link between the two.

3.) A good slogan drives people into action. Awakening triggers on the consumer's part will help make them the decision to buy the product being represented.

4.) A good slogan highlights the benefit of the product. This is tied up with the efforts of creating product distinction, which is to emphasize the benefits that one can derive from using a company's products or services.

**Advertising versus Business Slogan**

Business owners must be able to differentiate advertising from business slogans since they serve different purposes. The business slogan is more important since it concerns the brand identity. It impacts your distinction in the market and the power of your brand.

Meanwhile, advertising slogans are created for a specific marketing objectives and over a short-period of time. It is more concerned over influencing a consumer's immediate reaction to a given product while business slogan reinforces the reputation of a company as part of its branding efforts.

Brand Valuation For More Effective Marketing

What is Brand Valuation?

Over the years, brand valuation is being recognized as an important factor to be used in the analysis of marketing and finance efforts involved in the company. It falls under the intangible business assets category and is being closely looked into for ways to expand market share. Hence, many are undertaking new approaches that will boost efforts to increase the value of a given brand.

Since brand is a potent factor in every business, business owners are more interested in being able to translate that into financial terms. This is where brand valuation comes in. It is closely associated, if not directly related, to consumer perceptions about a brand and its list of products or services. However, aside from monetizing that value, business owners also utilize the impact of brand valuation as a way to determine areas that need to be improved to boost performance.

Determining Value of Brand

As a corporate asset, a brand is essential in helping increase the company's bottom line. If you can create a solid brand that increases your company's value to shareholders or consumers, then it will help increase your business potential. The concept of brand value remains quite hazy though, given the fact that no clear method has been established to measure exactly the value and worth of a given brand, especially because it is an intangible asset.

Still, there are a few who remains unconvinced as to what a brand really means. It could be the symbol that represents your company such as a name or logo. This then becomes a symbol for what the company stands for and promise to deliver. That definition of the brand is where value comes in as a brand is expected to deliver the expectations it has created to the consumers. To be able to do that takes commitment from the internal operations of the brand.

However, one cannot precisely give an exact value for a brand. There are direct and indirect processes involved though that enables a company to come up with a definite price for the brand, based on the investment put into developing it.

Direct Valuation Methods

To come up with a direct valuation method for a brand, it takes into account all investments put into the brand while also considering inflation. Other direct methods of value measurement used are Franchise Valuation and Awareness Valuation. When business owners plan on releasing a new product into the market, they typically include into the product value the advertising budget for that given product to increase awareness among consumers.

Indirect Valuation Methods

This is a more complicated process of determining the value of a brand than the one above. One process involves assessing the probable profit earnings that a particular brand is projected to produce. This method takes into consideration the effect that a brand has on the actual sales and profits acquisition. Another method also employs the use of the brand name in considering how one arrives with a value for the product.

Basically, all these methods are merely educated guesses to be able to account an efficient method for putting a price into the brand. Despite all existing debates about what the best method to use in computing brand value, or if brand value does offer any significant impact at all in the sales department, is something that will be settled only with the help of proper strategy. A brand is primarily not just a logo or name, but it is the set of values exhibited by your company for a consistent period.

So, as long as you have established the quality of your brand, then brand valuation should be easier to figure out.

# Building A Business Brand Through The Company Image

## Business and Image

In order to establish a strong business brand, you also need to create a strong business image. This will be used by potential customers or consumers to assess their own expectations about the company. There is a crucial moment in every marketing strategy that is aimed at attracting the customers' attention about your product and you achieve this through your company image and brand, which is also why it is of extreme importance.

More than any type of impression, you want to create a positive image on your customers. This will help ensure that you are among the top of their list when considering buying a product similar to yours. This is just the initial phase and eventually the confidence of your customers on your brand will soon come into play.

## Creating a Professional Logo

In the world of business, the logo represents who you are as a business. Hence, it should be able to capture and reflect the nature of your business at its most basic level. Identity and reputation should be followed thereafter.

As a reflection of your company, your objective is to design a logo with a professional touch because it is what creates the initial impression on the mid of the consumers. These first impressions are almost always impossible to undo, so you cannot risk coming up with a mediocre design. If you are unsure how to execute a design, it is always best to hire a professional to do it for you. This will help you attain a more consistent design for your logo that reinforces the message that your company is trying to convey. In fact, most businesses (big or small) allot an investment for this and you should as well.

As simple as it may sound, designing a logo is an intricate process, which is why you need a professional help realize your vision and visualize your business concepts. Among the elements that must be considered and combined effectively are colours, shapes, light, space, and so much more. Make sure to include this in your brand planning process.

Business Input Into The Design

Although you leave the designing job to the hands of a professional logo designer, this does not mean that you (the business owner) is eliminated from the formula. This is your business and it is your vision, therefore it is the most essential element in the logo creation process.

The process involves you gathering information and producing creative ideas that will be utilized by the designer in coming up with the design. Hence, careful planning and brainstorming of ideas is an essential step to take before jumping into the actual design process. You two must work in a symbiotic manner – you can share your business input to the designer for them to translate a graphic representation of your ideas, while they can propose designing elements that will jive with your business identity.

Where To Get Creative Ideas?

When dealing with the technical aspect of marketing strategy, often the challenge is to produce creative ideas for your design. The key here is to stimulate your brain to arouse creative thoughts that will make your brand stand out and still maintain that professional image.

Here are great tips you can try to squeeze out those creative juices:

1.) Spend time reading to be able to get inspiration from various reading materials.

2.) Search the web and observe various sites you visit. Look at how the design are produced and what kind of reaction it elicited on you.

3.) Ask your employees or other staffs for ideas. You can turn a small idea and develop it into a valid design concept.

Image is such a vital element in the business brand, which is why it is your main objective to create a professional design that is going to last.

Business Branding Strategies and Tips

Employing proper business branding strategies could spell the success for your business. Although it might be an intangible aspect of your business, it is basically what convinces people to buy or avail of your products or services. And when you garner enough sales, then only then can your business thrive.

What is a Branding Strategy?

A brand is not just a logo or a name, it represents your business identity. Therefore, it is a crucial part of the start-up process for any business. Branding strategies are employed to provide the fundamental steps and recognize the valuable tools that will help create a strong business brand. In general terms, a strong brand is one that people recognize and believe to deliver good quality. Have you ever found yourself at the grocery choosing one product over the other because it is the more recognized or trusted brand?

It is therefore a branding strategy's objective to recognize what could turn your business into a trusted brand name. How can you make people trust your brand and its reputation? What should you do to communicate the objective and mission of your company? What is the message you are trying to send out to produce loyal customers? A sound business branding strategy will aim to find answers to these questions before you can establish a brand for your company that would excel in the market.

## Create Name, Logo, or Website

Coming up with a name for your business goes hand in hand with creating a logo that will identify your company. When it comes to logos, always opt for something unique. Logos will be utilized in your advertising and marketing campaigns, so it must be well-recognized.

For beginners, think of a logo that will readily hint consumers about the nature of your business – such as whether you are in the food, automotive, or telecommunications business. Hence, choose images that are associated with the nature of your business and the products they will be used to represent.

## Slogan or Tagline

Once you have the logo that you want, you can think of a slogan that will reinforce the message you are trying to communicate to the consumers. As long as you keep this part brief and straightforward, then this can be an effective branding tool for your business. This tagline will serve as an additional touch to the main message you are trying to give, thus giving you an edge over your competitors and highlighting the unique experience or service that consumers will be able to avail of.

One advantage that you can get with including a tagline is that it is not permanent, unlike the logo. Therefore, if your company wishes to employ a new marketing strategy, you can readily change your tagline to highlight this new marketing ploy. A tagline then opens up several opportunities to expand your marketing campaigns, as compared to the static nature of company logos because they are the ones more difficult to establish.

## Colours and Images

As with logos, colours and images can be used to establish the identity of your business. Colours depict a corresponding set of emotions as well. Therefore, you need to carefully pick out exactly what type of colour you are going to use in your logo in accordance with the image and personality of your business. Try to conduct a little bit of research about the different qualities of colour types so you can determine exactly what best to use for your company.

## Unique Services

When communicating your company brand into the market, highlight the services that only you can offer. If you can guarantee a service that none of your competition can, then you create an edge on your customers over the same businesses. Then, you can use that as a chief marketing strategy to draw more people into your business. An example of this would be a time guarantee on your delivery services, if you're in the food business.

Learning how to effectively employ these business branding strategies will help boost your company's campaign and be that much closer to your desired business success.

Business Branding That Drive Sales

## Importance of Business Branding

Business branding is not just a one-time process. Rather, it is something you work on and build up over a period of time. After all, branding reflects your reputation as a business enterprise. Along with your efforts to create and manage your brand is the efforts of trying to build and protect your relationship with the customer base.

One of the best ways to establish the prominence of your brand in the market is by remaining consistent with the message that is conveyed by your marketing efforts. Refrain from claiming to produce bold and large scale promises. Your customers will easily remember when you fail to deliver in those promises. You could easily lose that reputation that took you years to build. Therefore, you need to pay attention to exactly what you need to do (and what not to do) if you want to turn that trust you have created amongst your customer base into increased sales.

## Campaign for Brand Awareness

Since every brand is distinct, you must also utilize varying approaches in communicating the brand's message across to its target market. This part entails immense creativity and a certain level of sensitivity to the needs of your prospected customers.

If you are not sure how to do this, you can take hint from other highly successful brands in the market. Study how they utilize their brand and what strategies they employ to get more people drawn into their brand. For instance, you can work on an emotional campaign, which is something that is rather difficult to do. But once you are able to establish that, then you could potentially increase your sales. One important thing to remember when you are using an emotional campaign is to always speak the truth about what your product is about and what it can do that will benefit your target market.

Tips for a Successful Emotional Campaign

If you decide that you want to appeal on your customer's emotion as your business branding strategy, then you need to consider various aspects that'll make it work. One way to effectively do that is share a story. This story could be fictional or not, but it should have some relation to the brand you are trying to campaign on. The idea here is to be able to produce some sort of personal improvement or progress by using the product.

If possible, base the emotional campaign on the brand itself, not just on the product. That way, you'd be able to produce a distinct campaign that will easily set you apart from competing companies. Then, whatever this message that you use in your campaign, try on remaining consistent with that. You can use different methods and campaign variations, but the message must remain the same in all of your brands.

After you have finalized your campaign, verify every bit of detail that is included in the campaign, whether you are using it for TV or print advertising.

Preserving Business Reputation

The brand recognition phase is over and now you have to utilize ways to preserve your company's reputation. It must involve taking notes and analyzing of your company's actions and how the customers perceive those actions, in relation to their satisfaction about your brand's performance and some other related factors.

Again, sensitivity to your customer's needs and using your brand to address that is one of the most effective measures toward business branding. As you go forward in your business efforts, try to learn more about effective business branding strategies to expand the reach of your brand in the market.

Business Name and Branding

Importance of a Business Name

An effective branding system starts with a great name. Unless you can put a name to your company that will distinguish it, you cannot proceed with creating a brand. It is similar to a newborn child, who must first be named before he or she can create their unique identity. Only then can you proceed with succeeding methods that are aimed at creating your mark in the market and enabling your business growth.

Creating a Name

Naming a company or brand is not as easy as naming a newborn child. Indeed, multiple factors come into play such as producing a name with a good recall on the consumers, the type of product you have in your business, its features and usage, and other benefits that consumers can experience from using it. That is just one aspect of what you need to consider when naming your product or brand.

The other end of the formula requires you to envision yourself in the mindset of the consumers. How is the product useful to me? And what benefits can I get from using it? Add to that all other competing businesses that offer the same product as you do. These are all pointers you need to look into if you want to get a share of the market and increase sales production.

**Do's and Don'ts**

Creating a business name can be confusing sometimes, either for lack or excess of ideas that make it difficult filtering them out. Below are a few tips you should consider when naming a business:

• Opt for memorable and catchy names instead of generic ones that are difficult to register in the minds of the consumers.

• Never use names that literally describes the product. Go for creative ones.

• If possible, do not use geographical names because it limits the scope of your business. However, this is an advantage if your product is associated with a given locale or affinity.

• Refrain from restrictive names to save you from trouble in the future in case you want to expand your line of business.

• Keep them short so as to produce memorable names.

## Name as Part of Branding Strategy

A business name is not just a name; it represents your business identity. And in the business community, the way you represent and project your image is crucial in determining success. This is because perceptions, more than the actual value of the product or services, is essential in helping consumers decide on whether to buy that product or not. On top of the brand itself, it makes association with the company and its reputation. That is why most businesses spend and invest most of their efforts on building a trusted business reputation that will strengthen the trust of consumers on their company.

Your business name essentially determines how far your company will go in this endeavour. When people encounter your business or brand, you have only a meagre amount of time to catch their attention. If you fail to do so, then you would have lost a potential customer. More than just intriguing, a good business name is one that compels your target market. If you can produce one, then it will surely catapult your business to your desired commercial success.

A good business name is not just a superficial aspect involved in branding but rather a legitimate business factor that must be taken into consideration.

## Colour Coordinated Business Branding

Image is a vital factor in any business branding effort. Colour is part of the process of building an image. If you might notice, several top businesses are recognized by their distinct colours. Therefore, you need to realize the potential impact that carefully choosing the colour to use as part of your brand strategy will help establish your company's image amongst consumers.

### Importance of Colour

Although it might seem trivial, colour affects the memory recall of consumers on your product or company overall. When they think of a certain colour similar to the ones used by your company brand, then they will easily associate that colour with your product. The presence of colour will then stimulate one's senses and sending message signals without having to initiate a communicative pattern.

Now that you know the role that colour plays in your brand strategy, the next big dilemma is choosing the colour to use. However, even this one shouldn't be as difficult provided that you have clearly set out the guidelines and vision you have for the company. Once you have chosen the colour, you must then use that in all of your business promotional materials to further enhance the prominence of the colour in association with your company and its products or services.

Each colour have its universal meaning that you must take into account before using them in your business branding efforts. Here are basic colours to consider:

## Blue

The colour blue, universally speaking, is a well-liked colour. It exudes a feeling of trustworthy, responsibility, and security. That is why blue is also commonly used in the business industry because it is not only pleasant to look at, but it exudes a positive vibe as it is a colour associated with the sea and sky. The message of stability conveyed by the use of this colour builds up trust among individuals working within an institution.

## Red

Another popular colour used in several brand of company. The colour red stimulates your senses rapidly, hence it is an attention grabbing colour that creates the impression of being aggressive and energetic. This colour is utilized by businesses who want to evoke emotion and quick response from potential customers. Fast food chains typically use the colour red because it exhibits a hot, burning and intensify attitude.

## Green

In terms of its universal meaning, green connotes health and serenity. But the meaning can differ though according to the shades of green used.

Lighter shades of green produce a calming effect while darker ones exude wealth and prestige.

Yellow

This is a colour closely associated with the sun. Therefore, it is a colour that you might want to use if you want to establish a positive message of optimism and warmth. There are also varying shades for this colour but their meaning ranges from creating motivation to producing positive energy. Bright yellows effectively captures the eyes, so you might want to use this colour for displays and you can get people's attention, which is the first step in every purchase process.

Black

This is a classic choice of colour for a business brand. Aside from that, it also connotes a bold, powerful, and sophisticated persona. Therefore, this colour is quite common for expensive products or most sophisticated gadgets.

White

As always, white signifies simplicity and purity. Because any white object produce a certain level of brightness, it is good for use on signages. The same with black, it also helps you achieve a professional and powerful image. This colour is best associated with products relating to health and sanitary care.

Use all these pointers when choosing a colour for use on your business branding strategy and you will be able to produce more impact on your marketing campaigns.


Common Branding Mistakes and Myths To Avoid

What Makes a Brand Identity?

Branding is an aspect of every business that consists of visual elements and are used for the company's marketing purposes. Therefore, most business owners would hire a professional logo designer to execute the concepts laid out by the company, which they believe will help communicate the company's business into the market. This logo will then be used as a marketing material that will appear on business cards, envelopes, letterheads, or other professionally related materials.

Establishing the brand identity is one of the initial steps that must be taken by a company if it wishes to achieve market success. Hence, this process must involve careful brand planning and though to avoid damaging your business. You must also look into how the customers might perceive the message being delivered by your brand, to avoid having it work against you.

Designing the Brand

There is no need to reiterate the importance of your brand identity to the success of your business. Therefore, this is an area of your business planning and start-up that must be left to the professionals, especially if you are new to the business industry.

Although you might have a sense of creativity, graphic designing becomes an entirely different concept when it is associated with using it as a marketing tool.

Apart from being creative and visually appealing, the brand logo must have meaning and is able to convey essential information about your company. Here are some benefits you can get from hiring a professional to design your logo:

*The creation of your brand logo will serve as priority. Hence, you are able to set a specific time-frame for the completion of the job to ensure that it is being focused on closely.
*As a professional logo designer, it is their job to utilize their unique skills as a graphic designer and incorporate their expertise on the importance of logo in relation to the marketing side of your business.

Customizing Brand Design

Contrary to popular belief, designing your own company logo to use as marketing material is not expensive. But of course this is relative, especially if you insist on using high-quality materials for this but this is totally your own preference should you have enough budget for this. If not, then a sound concept and a skilled logo designer will be able to produce a strong brand.

After all, this is a business investment since your brand can impact your sales. This is a relatively inexpensive investment with a potential for a lucrative profit.

## Understanding the Importance of Branding

Several businessmen tend to neglect the creation of a brand identity. Therefore, most of them fail in their business endeavours and yet they do not even realize where the lapses are coming from. A brand identity is as essential as some of the basic priorities in every business start-up such as a business name, bank account, or operating system. And if ever a brand is created, most business owners do not look into the details of the brand and thus ending up with a brand that misrepresent their company.

Below is a list of common branding mistakes that must be avoided:

• Failure to create an efficient brand planning.

• Not giving full commitment to the management and review of the brand.

• Inability to establish internal branding.

• Lack of a sound marketing plan.

• Trying way too hard to create distinction to the point of inaccessibility.

Branding your business is never easy but once you recognize the factors that could impede your business' progress, then you're on your way there.

# Branding in a Troubled Economy

A good business brand is one that can withstand an ailing economy. In today's times wherein majority of the world is suffering from financial crisis, small-to big-time businesses are feeling the impact of this downturn.

This is when your branding campaign will be put to the test. Indeed, when businesses are competing for what remains of the market, you have to double your efforts at making the brand enable your business to thrive. What is also essential in these times is to never discount the impact of quality and improving value statements. These are important factors that hold promise to deliver more to the clients and keep your business afloat.

Are You Recession-Proof?

Branding seems to lose its vigour during recession. People tend to buy base on logic and needs, rather than impulse or perceptions. Therefore, you have to maintain or improve the kind of value, property, and benefits that your product promises its consumers. This is something that you must not lose focus on in your branding and marketing efforts, but its significance become more evident during times of recession.

If you want to add more value to your brand to make it better able to withstand the challenges of a suffering economy, here are areas of your branding system that must be given focus on:

• During recession, most businesses would tend to cut back on their marketing efforts and investments. On the contrary, this is the time wherein you need to strengthen your marketing efforts.

• Create more aggressive marketing programs to be able to capture a bigger share of the market.

• Assert yourself on consumers largely affected by recession by offering better value on your products.

• Your advertising campaign must highlight quality, economic benefits, and real benefits as opposed to appeal to their superficial concerns.

## Helping Your Brand Survive The Recession

When recession has hit the consumers, buying becomes a less desirable practice. This will largely impact your business' efforts and this is made worse by the intensity of competition amongst various similar businesses.

Try using the following practices to keep your business thriving:

1.) Never change your brand identity. Doing so will reduce the trust you have built on the customers and will also ruin your reputation. Merely try to restructure the messages you are trying to deliver but make sure that it stays within the context of your basic brand identity.

2.) Utilize this time to appeal to your customer's needs by performing a more thorough market research. This will produce an impression that you are concerned about their needs and are seeking for ways to deliver that.

3.) If your business' products are mostly high-end, do not simply revert to dropping prices. Instead, try improving the value and quality of your products so that customers will have a better quality spending habit.

4.) Be open to potential new customers. In times of recession, people are in the process of re-evaluating their spending habits. This is your opportunity to come into the picture and offer your business as a possible solution.

## Ensuring Brand Stability

Consumers change their buying patterns during recession, but business owners must remain committed with their branding strategies. However, you do have to make slight and appropriate changes though, such as increased sensitivity to this new buying attitude exhibited by consumers. During times of recession, you have to stay committed in helping your customers attain quality service and products that add more value to their money. This is your winning formula.

And with increased dedication to your business brand, you will also increase the loyalty of your patrons.

# Creating A Strong Business Brand

Creating a business brand is one thing, but creating a strong business brand is another. Therefore, every starting businessman needs to be aware of the fundamentals involved in creating a business brand that would enable your product to excel in the market. However, you must not be scared by this process; instead, try to enjoy the exercise of brand building and you will be able to build a brand that you can be proud of and your customers will love.

## Focus on the Business

Before even thinking of a brand, think first of your business. After all, the brand is merely a representative of your business. So, you must refrain from focusing too much on developing an effective brand without giving attention to the business. Your brand must come as a result of your business, not the other way around.

Therefore, you need to come up with your band depending on the following factors:

*nature of business
*type of service to customers
*distinction from competitors

## Nature of Business

One of the purpose of creating a brand is to communicate to the consumers what your company does. Therefore, take time to evaluate the nature of your business and the distinct attributes and images it tries to convey to the market. If possible, try to produce your brand according to the specific target market that you are aiming for your business. Is your business catering to mothers, young adults, or children? This will help establish the name and image for your business.

Once you increase awareness of your brand as a representative of your company's products or services, only then can you expect to experience increased sales. Therefore, creating a firm brand that will be easily remembered and distinct will enable you to create a loyal customer base.

Type of Service

The entailing concept surrounding a brand name such as a logo, strapline, mission statement, or color scheme are all but abstract concepts. What establishes a brand as a concrete representation for your company and business is the experience that your customer has with your product or service. Therefore, you need to establish that relationship between your customer and the kind of service you bring to them as one aspect that will enable your brand to establish itself in the memory of your customer.

Indeed, perceived value of your company is a vital formula that would produce a strong business brand. It is not all about images but delivering to the emotional and physical needs of your customer will help reinforce your brand's campaign in the market.

## Distinction From Competition

Although examining the type of brand that are utilized by your competitors will help you establish your own brand, you need to differentiate from them while exceeding them at the same time. Distinction must not only arise from the business name or logo itself, but in terms of the quality of service that you deliver. What can you offer that your competitors have not and cannot offer customers? Then, incorporate that into the creation of your brand so you will easily be able to capture customer's attention as to the possibility of doing business with you.

In a market that is flooded with several other businesses, making yourself unique and distinct from others is one way to establish the reputation of your business. Couple that with a passion for delivering top-notch customer and quality service, you are sure to establish a strong business brand that will help your company achieve its goals.

Creating A Powerful Message With A Potent
Branding System

Your Brand's Mission

The basic framework of an efficient branding
system is a vision. Vision is translated into a brand
and that brand is utilized in various communication
methods to deliver a message to the market and the
consumers. That is how the process works. But in
reality, it is not as simple as it sounds or appear.
There are several variables involved that could end
up you sending the wrong message. Hence, you
need to constantly evaluate the branding system you
use to ensure that you are communicating your
company's message effectively.

Every company nowadays desire to build a strong
brand, because it is after all what helps one produce
profits and build a loyal customer base. But what
most companies often fail to realize is that brands
are avenues to showcase the mission of the
organization. Although some companies who fail to
do this experience some level of commercial
success, those who give much attention to utilizing
their brand as a means to deliver their mission is
one that is able to withstand the challenges and
downturns of the marketing industry.

## The Purpose of Brand

You can exert your effort on the creation of a logo,
name, or design for your company, but the essence
behind them is what is truly important in every
business branding system. It is not just one of these
elements but rather a combination of them all. But

how will the market be able to create that distinction about your company against other companies if you cannot foster it to deliver a message?

The brand holds immense power over your company since it is what customers utilize to create perceptions about the company which the brand represents. Therefore, branding is not something that is restricted to large scale companies and be given attention to, but it is basically for all levels of businesses.

## Steps Towards a Brand Strategy

If you want to arrive at a cost-efficient strategy, your first order of business is to get into the mind of your potential customers. This must be given much attention to when doing your market research. Gather as much information about your customer demographics that you can utilize in the development of your brand. But do not simply settle for that; instead, learn more about what factors would encourage them or prompt them to act on the impulse to heed the message being delivered by your brand. This is the part wherein you tailor your message based on what appeals to the emotional and physical needs of the consumers.

The word-of-mouth is one of the most effective yet cheap advertising tool that you can utilize within your company. Hence, you need to gather ideas on how you can produce a brand that will have people talk about it and convince others to respond to the message of your brand.

# Internal Branding

In whatever type of brand strategy you employ, you must focus on remaining consistent with the overall vision and objectives of the company. This also helps build a stronger level of trust among your customers about the reputation of your company.

Therefore, you need to hire and develop people who understand the importance of the core values exhibited in the company's vision and objectives. Having people within your company who realize exactly what the brand wants to showcase to people, then you are more capable of producing a cohesive and consistent message to the market about what your brand is about. This will also help ensure that you can deliver the promises of the company as part of your branding system.

## Effect of Word-of-Mouth Marketing on Your Branding Strategy

### Word of Mouth Marketing

There's probably no more effective branding strategy in existence than word of mouth marketing. However, only few realize its actual potential in helping you build a successful business and branding system. What could be better than having actual people talk others into doing business with your company? It is a common thing for people to do, which is talk about something a recent product that they were satisfied or had good experiences with.

And yet, word of mouth marketing does not cost you anything. It is just as effective as other methods of advertising or increasing awareness about your company's products or services but without the entailing costs and investments. Even marketing experts profess word of mouth marketing to be the most potent means of communicating a company's marketing message.

Effects of Word of Mouth Marketing

If you have seen various TV commercials or websites that sell products, then you might already be familiar with testimonials. This is a marketing ploy utilized by most business owners in order to provide a valid proof with regards to the benefits and claims made by the company, which is in the form of actual users of the product.

However, there is a discrepancy here: if business owners were to tap people to provide a testimony about a product and the results experienced, then it is most likely a biased demographic. The business owner will pick only users who have something positive to say about the product, since their main intent is to influence the buying choices of the consumers.

This is when the power of word of mouth marketing becomes evident. Using this method to communicate the potentials of a given brand creates a personal connection between the consumers and the product in question. Previous users to the product who attained satisfaction from it can recommend the product to their friends or family members. Therefore, business owners can get free advertisement out of that, which is probably as effective (or more) than a TV ad but without the costs.

Word of mouth marketing can work to a company's disadvantage as well. It happens when people who have tried the product have certain complaints about bad service, or bad quality products, and unsatisfactory customer relations. Research reveals that word of mouth marketing essentially has a bigger impact on the buying decisions of people aged between 18 to 34 and 35-54.

Bigger Customer Voice

It has been highly emphasized by marketing experts that if you want to maintain or increase your market share, you need to work on providing excellent customer service. This will ensure that you get a share of loyal customers who believe and trust in your brand. If you're able to successfully enhance that trust, then you are able to produce a good customer voice. Therefore, when these individuals are asked to say something about your company, they only have positive views to say.

Hence, several companies are now devising methods to improve their "listening" ability when it comes to customer voice. Indeed, improving customer communications will produce satisfied customers and consequently increase the potential of producing more positive word of mouth marketing.

Tips for Increasing Word of Mouth Marketing

A recent study conducted to determine the most influential marketing methods, word of mouth marketing came out on top. Hence, it has raised awareness on the important role that consumers play in influencing other's buying options. Therefore, you can utilize a positive word of mouth marketing to create your own sound branding strategy. Here's how you can do it:

• Create a branding strategy that will get people interested and have them talk about it. Unless you can arouse their curiosity and attention, you will not succeed in this.

• See to it that you satisfy customer needs. When people are happy about your product, they will joyfully and willingly recommend it to others.

• Respond to feedbacks, whether positive or negative. Aside from promoting your business, you can utilize word of mouth marketing as a means to gather essential information on how you can improve your service and branding strategy.

Elements of an Effective Business Brand

Building a Business Brand

No business brand is produced overnight. It follows a methodical process that involves strategy and organization. But if you think that once you have a business name and logo that your work is already done, then you need to know that even with long-standing business the process of brand management is still ongoing. Aside from time, some big companies even invest lots of time and amount just to ensure that the legacy of the brand remains consistent to the values embodied by the company.

Small-time business owners can take comfort in the fact that building a brand need not be expensive. All you need is commitment to the process to provide a focus and consistency on your branding efforts. There are four elements involved in producing a successful business brand.

Consistent Message

One of the best way to achieve a consistent marketing approach is to create a unified name, logo, and image. This is one of the most efficient ways that you can communicate what your business is about to your potential customers. Therefore, you need to bear in mind about the vision and mission of your company, which is initially the inspiration behind the design of the logo. Then, you need to use that in relation with what marketing strategies you employ to promote your brand image and increase awareness.

Even when you come up with innovative marketing ideas to reinvent your image or offer customers something new, it has to remain true to the ideals of your business.

Brand Planning

Careful brand planning is essential in building a strong business brand. Regardless of what marketing methods you utilize to enhance brand awareness, you need to look into each detail that is involved with the process. This helps ensure that you are able to achieve consistency, which is a crucial element indicated above.

You need to identify what branding strategies will enable you to achieve your goals. If it does not work, what back-up plans do you have? All marketing efforts are aimed towards strengthening your brand to gain a return of investment.

Branding System

This is the part wherein you put into action everything you have designed during brand planning. Different systems must be employed for every phase involved in the overall business and brand development. It must properly outline what steps you and your employees must take during certain circumstances. Bear in mind that a holistic and integrated system is key in creating a strong brand.

Review and Management

Every brand must continually undergo a review process. Since consumers' needs and demands change, so must your brand's marketing approach. Here are aspects of the brand review and management procedures that you must take into account:

• Product benefits and features

• Market competition

• Changing customer needs and demands

• Marketing methods used

Continued evaluation of these factors in relation to your brand's marketing strategies will help produce a more efficient and cohesive marketing efforts. You will have brand managers to look into the welfare of the brand and what methods are to be executed to enhance its market performance. However, internal branding is still of importance since they are the ones that are responsible for delivering these products or services.

So, it is therefore important that they are aware about the business brand's objectives as well.

Essential Tips for Effective Business Branding

When a businessman embark on a new business venture, they readily go processing ideas on complicated marketing strategies and other ways of promoting their business but none of their efforts are dedicated to business branding. Indeed, with so much factors coming into play, it is easy to miss out on the most essential and basic aspect. But that is just one half of it, since the other half is dedicated into ensuring that you can build an effective brand that will produce results for your marketing efforts.

But the key to an effective branding strategy is to be able to deliver. You must be able to back up your claims and produce exactly as you say. Majority of your business sales and profits come from repeat customers, after all. An effective business branding system involves the following:

Customer Satisfaction

Brand is just a mere representation of your company. Therefore, it must reflect exactly what your business can deliver for the customers and build its reputation from there. If you cannot produce quality product or services, then regardless of how potent your branding system or strategies are, you'd never be able to turn your marketing campaigns into a sales force.

Therefore, you need to be as sensitive to your customers' needs as possible. But only to a certain extent that you still hold control over the image and reputation that you want your brand to exhibit.

Indeed, brand equity is a vital aspect in every business, especially consumer-based equity. It reflects the level of trust and attitude that a customer has towards a product associated with a given brand. This is impacted by the actual experience that a consumer has had with the product such that brand loyalty is affected by factors such as perceived quality and the delivery of the product.

Consistency

One of the most effective ways to build trust amongst your customers is to be consistent with the message you are trying to convey. Consistency is most important when exhibiting the values that are key and vital in your company. Then, focus on every aspect of your business to ensure that it remains consistent with the values professed by your company and that they make a good representation of the company's vision.

Expanding Your Brand

Creating a brand for your company is not only limited to the creation of a logo. While it is essential, your work does not stop there. After all, a logo is just a representation of your professional image but there are several factors in between that would help translate them into sales. You do not even have to spend lots of money to fulfill them. In every form of communication that you use in your business transactions, include your company logo in it, whether you'd be using business cards, yellow page ads, newsletters, letterhead, invoices, envelopes, and many more. Your logo is of no use unless you are able to capitalize on it and make it do its work for you.

Managing Your Brand

As market trends continue to change and evolve, so must your approach at branding strategies. While you set your own company's branding standards, you also need to look into exceeding those promises you've set and this is one of the most effective ways to generate more customers. On the other end, one failure could eventually ruin your business' reputation on a long haul.

If you see any opportunity where changes can be done or improvements can be executed, then don't be afraid to execute them. This is one way for your business to stay on top of things and keep up with changing trends in the market for an effective business branding effort.

Expanding Your Business Branding Online

Promoting business branding online is similar and
yet different from typical marketing strategies.
Therefore, you have to make unique approach to
this method of promoting your business brand. And
yet, the benefits of using web tools in making your
brand distinct includes the ability to maximize your
business efforts and expanding your business' reach.
After all, it only makes sense to extend your
branding efforts to the internet given the fact that
most people nowadays use the internet as their
source of daily information.

There are five major areas that you need to address
when developing a strong business brand online.

URL Address

This is a crucial determiner for web browsers.
Therefore, you must be able to produce a sense of
identity for your website and provide a glimpse into
your company even before they get the opportunity
to see what your website is really about.

Keywords

The keywords are essential to help search engines
connect you to the proper audience. Use keywords
that are related to the nature of your website, so that
it can be easily detected when people run a search
on the internet. Try to be creative in coming up with
keywords to use, especially those queries not
directly related but associated to your business.

## Website

This is where you get to showcase your company's vision and your offer of quality products or services. Therefore, you must create a website that speaks for your brand. There are several ways to do that, which includes the content, style, design, and color. You must also incorporate your company logo in the design of the website, to enhance the level of trust and confidence on the consumers to your website. Therefore, you must refrain from compromising the substance of your website for style. A website is just another form of marketing strategy and its objective is to communicate your company's message.

## Weblog

Your blog is basically where you focus on producing quality content. This will help establish your company's brand as something that is of authority to sell a given service or product. There are several spammers that infiltrate the online community, so you have to separate yourself from them. You can do this by remaining consistent with your vision and highlighting your focus on producing a quality brand.

## Social Profiles

There are several social networking sites online such as Twitter, LinkedIn, Facebook, among others. When you join any one of these social sites, always include your company signature or brand representative such as a logo. This will help visitors to easily remember your company and be on top of their list.

Business Branding Online Do's and Dont's

• Utilizing social network sites that you are interested in as an avenue to promote your brand online is beneficial for your business. Here, you can make connections and expand the reach of your brand. Getting more people into your page will produce major brand building traffic into your site.

• Just write useful and quality content on your site. When people begin to realize the importance of your site's content, it will eventually impact your performance on search engines.

• Try to offer advice or solution to the needs of the people. But refrain from spamming since it would basically ruin your business' reputation.

Business branding online has expanded the reach of your branding efforts to produce a more promising growth for your company.

## How Can You Measure A Brand?

### Measuring a Brand

Every business involves its own share of tangible and intangible assets, but brand is one of the most basic areas that business owners focus on. In a recent marketing research, it was revealed that brand equity played a vital role in determining its market value. Therefore, measuring a brand is one of the first steps undertaken by the head of the company if they wish to incur higher revenues.

### How To Measure?

There are several elements involved in trying to measure a brand and its market value. All these factors intersect with one another such that they impact one another in evaluating the importance of a given brand and its value in the market. There are several variables involved such as whether you are weighing more importance on pricing or is more interested in enlarging your share of the market. That is something that you need to figure out amongst your organization first. Then, you can take into account the following brand value measures to reach your desired goals.

### Price Premium

You need to evaluate your own brand and put yourself in the mindset of the consumers. How much are you willing to pay for that brand? Most recognized brands typically place higher premiums on their product as compared to other similar products from unknown brands. There are several marketing aspects to consider here but you can establish your brand by trying to lower your price to get a bigger share of the market. You have to conduct a thorough market research though before you come up with any decisions, so you have a basis for your evaluation.

Customer Satisfaction

To come up with a tangible data about this, you might have to conduct a survey. This will enable you to track down goods or services that appeal most to consumers. You can also take note whether there are any repeat purchases. This will enable you to effectively measure your brand's value in the market.

Perceived Quality

Based on the level of satisfaction and benefits derived from the use of the product, consumers will have their varying perceptions when it comes to the quality of a given product. But even this one entails several variables such as consistency of delivering quality products or its performance in comparison to competition.

Perceived Value

There are two ways to look into this one: in terms of money and benefits. However, these two are interlaced. Meaning, consumers determine the value of a product for its money based on whether it delivers the kind of benefits that the product promised and the consumers expect from it.

## Organization's Reputation

Even though it is not directly concerned with the product that a customer is in the process of buying, the reputation of the company behind the product impacts their buying choices. Is it a credible organization? Is it something that I can trust? Building that reputation comes in part of a business' effort to build a strong brand.

## Awareness

To achieve this, most businesses often work on establishing brand recognition. Brand recall oftentimes lead to purchases since most buyers opt to buy something that is familiar to them, as opposed to an unknown product or brand. You need to work on protecting your brand though as a few mistake can destroy the brand that you have built.

Establishing a value for your brand proves to be difficult and a lot of hard work. And yet, money is only a meager factor in the entire formula. Only when a brand has established itself well enough such that consumers are willing to pay for it, regardless of the price, does it achieve its true value as a brand.

Impact of Internal Branding In Your Marketing Efforts

## About Internal Branding

Most companies focus entirely on promoting their brand to create a positive perception on the consumer's brand that internal branding loses its share of the formula. An important share, at that. Marketing efforts are executed to establish a high-quality brand that delivers to the needs and demands of the consumers. But how do you ensure that you are delivering up to the standards of your company? This is where internal branding comes into play.

To attain good quality products and services for your brand, you need to take care of your business' internal processes first. Internal branding is about the focus you give on ensuring that practices and methods utilized in the creation of products or services meet your company's set of values. Branding must be done inside and out. You need to be able to reproduce these values in the mind of everyone who is a part of the organization so you can naturally promote your brand.

## How Do You Achieve It?

You cannot produce a good marketing message to the public unless you start from within. That is something every business owner need to realize. Therefore, you need to learn strategies as to how you can effectively execute a sound internal branding system to ensure a cohesive take on developing a brand that will satisfy your potential customers.

Here's how you can do it:

• Gather together all of your development team work together in the development and creation of the brand to ensure that all methods are synchronized with your values and set of objectives laid out by the company.

• When hiring employees to work with you, choose those that are aligned with the corporate values of your company. Having the right set of skills will enable you to achieve the most effective brand representation you desire.

• Keep internal communication lines open at all times. This will enable you to reinforce and enhance whatever existing values that are being executed to meet the promise of your brand. If you keep nurturing this in the mind of the employees, then they will be able to develop that soon enough.

Benefits of Internal Branding

Aside from unity in your company's vision towards what you want to achieve with your brand, internal branding offers more benefits. If you are not aware of the potential benefits that internal branding offers, these are just a few ways that it can help boost your brand's campaign:

• Internal branding produces a healthy working environment and cohesive working culture. Once all employees understand the vision behind the brand, all components of the company are now geared towards the same goals.

• Internal branding produces a more consistent branding message. Once your brand have established a given brand reputation, your employees will be proud to represent your company while at the same time be challenged to meet its set of standards.

• Internal branding serves as an avenue to push for change.

• Internal branding develops your brand identity.

Basic Principles

If you want to create an effective internal branding system, every company must give attention to the following set of principles:

1.) Give freedom not control. An effective internal branding management is one that emphasizes a set of rules that are agreed on by the employees, so they could genuinely contribute to the advancement of your brand.

2.) Decentralize. Learn how to trust your employees to deliver the quality your brand deserves.

3.) Communicate your company's message to the personnel first before the customers. How do you expect your employees to deliver the type of standard you want to achieve if they do not have proper understanding of the company's objectives?

4.) Synchronized operation. You need to be able to pull together different departments of the company so that everyone works at the same pace and perspective.

5.) Think long-term goals. No brand is created overnight. Therefore, you need to create that mindset in your personnel that enables them to think of the long-term impacts and effects of an effective internal branding system.

# Importance of Branding Your Business

## What is a Brand?

Branding your business is an essential step that any business owner need to take, whether yours is a small- or big-time business. In fact, it is something that must be looked into during the phase of business planning.

A brand is basically a name or a logo that will be used in advertising campaigns to represent your company or business. This will be used when printing out your business cards or when referring to your company. Hence, deciding on a brand must be undertaken with much consideration and thought. To sum it up, a brand details who you are, what you do, and how you do it.

## Importance of Branding

There are several aspects that involve branding businesses. Each has its own importance and impact on attaining your business goals. This is a step that every beginning businessman needs to educate him or herself about because it will determine the company's performance in the future.

Here are reasons as to why business branding must be given careful thought:

Creating Business Identity

When you use a business idea to start your own business venture, chances are there are already some other existing businesses with the same nature as yours. Therefore, you need to create a brand for your business that will differentiate you from your competitors.

So when deciding on a brand name or logo for your company, you need to think of creative ways that will help make your business be easily remembered by potential customers. Distinction is a vital part of every business venture and when people find that you have something unique to offer that lets you stand out from competing businesses, then you are one step closer to your business goals.

Once you have created your company brand, then that is when you need to look into delivering quality product or service that your brand will be perceived as. That takes you now to the next essential aspect involved with branding, which is marketing.

Marketing and Advertising Campaigns

Branding also impacts the sales force of your product. If you are able to create a brand name that people will easily remember and recognize for your outstanding products, then it helps create an efficient branding system for your company.

The first step for a successful business is taking the time to let people know who you are, what you do, and the means at which you do it. Properly communicating your company's vision through your brand is an essential stage of any business branding effort. Having established an effective company brand will also create awareness of the product you are promoting.

So, when people hear your brand, then they would easily think of your products or services and your company's reputation.

## What is Brand Credibility?

Brand credibility is often pointed out by marketing experts as one psychological factor that could trigger the buying impulse of consumers. However, just like with any type of triggers, it can produce a positive or negative effect. In this case, it refers to your brand's reputation and its ability (or inability) to convert that into sales.

As a business owner, you must try to change your perspective into that of the consumers. Try to understand how you would perceive various companies and how it affects your buying decisions. Most often, consumers would opt for those companies that are deemed to be experts in their respective industries.

Other factors that affect your buying patterns would include longevity, which covers the years that a company has been in existence. This reflects their mass appeal and quality of their service or product given that it has been patronized by a certain demographic and for that given period. This is what credibility in branding is about: the perception that people have of your business or company.

Establishing Credibility

Now that you understand what brand credibility is, you must face the harder question: how do you establish it? This is even more difficult for business newcomers or business startups because there is a lot of work to be done. Aside from that, you need to continually nourish it so as to be able to maintain that credibility that you have built up for your business.

Credibility is the heart of every business. Even though you offer quality products or services, if your customers perceive your company as incapable of delivering such level of quality, then it would be of no use. It would not be able to confirm your business as a reliable choice among several possible competing choices in the market.

To produce brand credibility, you need to meet the following categories:

• Non-verbal such as your logo or image,

• Verbal efforts through marketing or advertising,

• Mission and Vision of the business to exemplify your organization's values,

• and, Internal operations that is crucial in delivering your promises to the customer.

Following are tips on how you can build credibility towards success.

## Customer Perceptions

You establish this initially by doing business that satisfies your customer. When you make advertisement claims about your product or service, you need to meet or exceed their expectation standards to be able to build that positive perception about your company. First impressions always last, so you need to make a good first impression if you want to increase market share.

## Highlight Business Competence

Regardless of what product or service you are offering, you must demonstrate your expertise in that given field. Show data and statistics that serve as proof to what your company is capable of delivering. That is why most companies or websites advertise with testimonials to prove the results of using their product. When consumers see actual results, it extends from your products to your overall company image.

## Consistency

As already mentioned above, establishing credibility is not a one-time process. Instead, you must also work on maintaining and enhancing it. After all, one mistake could easily trump the reputation you have built. Consistency then becomes of utmost importance in your business. It must be aligned with all processes involved in your business operations, from advertising, to the marketing, and production.

If you want to attain a certain level of standard, it must be true for all levels of business operation since this will serve to back up your integrity. Learn to follow the essentials of building and establishing brand credibility for it is one important aspect in achieving longevity.

# Increasing Brand Recognition For Improved Sales

## About Brand Recognition

In any form of marketing strategy, brand recognition is usually the initial focus. Business owners employ varying tactics to increase familiarity on their brand wherein the ultimate aim is to create awareness about the existence of a given product or service. This process will then produce a domino effect and impacts people trust of the product and their decision on whether to purchase it or not.

Brand recognition can be achieved through various means though. Which is a good thing for business owners because this means they do not have to allot large amounts of money in order to get their brand recognized in the market. Awareness is of the essential in all efforts for brand recognition. All other steps needed to be taken after that must be looked at a different aspect, but this one serve its own purpose.

Importance of Brand Recognition

The reason might seem obvious but brand
recognition offers multiple benefits for your
business. It is capable of impacting other aspects of
your business, hence this is a crucial determiner for
success. Some experts have claimed that brand
recognition is the most important factor that could
spell a business' success potential.

However, the main importance of brand recognition
is to establish a mental connection between your
business and its potential customers. Therefore,
when your prospects hear about your company or its
name, they will be able to produce a general idea of
what products and services your business is
offering.

With several similar business available, creating a
distinction for your name in a given field of
business will encourage more people to do business
with you. You also need to consider the
psychological aspect of it. Studies have revealed
that people tend to go for a name that they know or
recognize. So, this is a helpful stat that you need to
take advantage of.

How To Increase Visibility?

If you've been working on a business start-up, then
chances are you already know the importance of
brand recognition and its role in the success of your
business. But the bigger question remains: how do
you do it? Traditional marketing efforts for most
company involves major expenditures being set

aside for increasing media presence such as advertisement, to increase awareness of the product and create a connection between consumers.

Today, there are a lot more avenue for that, in fact more interactive ones. Aside from the traditional media outlets, the internet has opened up several possibilities to enable a business to establish its name and potentially grow. Therefore, companies have also worked on increasing their web presence to expand their market reach.

Studies have shown that most web surfers begin with a search. Therefore, it is best to optimize your web site in such a way that it ranks well in the search engines. In short, you have to make efforts to make your website easily found by potential web researchers. That is why several companies invest in search engine optimization to improve their performance and marketing strategies on the web.

Producing Strong Brands

The impact of brand recognition extends beyond purely marketing but also appeals to the emotion of the consumers. In order to produce a strong brand that has established itself on the industry, you must be able to purge favorable emotions from your customers. It is one thing that largely impacts a consumer's buying decision, so it pays to invest in an effective brand recognition strategy.

The good thing about brand recognition is that it is not limited to giant companies. It also offers substantial benefits for even small-scale businesses. As the the cliché goes, familiarity breeds comfort.

And when people have increased familiarity or brand recognition, then they are most likely to feel confident about using your products.


## Managing and Reviewing Your Business Brand

Effective establishment and management of your business brand is as equally difficult as creating one. Indeed, one's you have created a standard and built your own company's reputation, then you would have to constantly live up to that standard and avoid under-delivering. In the business industry, a failure for your company can produce manifold consequences and if you want to protect the brand you worked so hard on building, then you need to continually check on every aspect of it.

## Managing Your Business Brand

If possible, assign a person who will continually look into the management of your company's brand strategy. After all, it is a vital aspect of your business that you need to protect if you want to maintain whatever market success your business is currently enjoying. If not, then you can educate your employees or staffs on exactly what are the missions and objectives of your company brand. This knowledge will help them become aware of their role in producing and meeting customer's standards for your business.

If you are aiming for a certain standard, having all members of your crew working towards the same goal and at the same pace will enrich all your efforts for an effective branding strategy. For a more effective management scheme, ask for suggestions on their end as well. You can get valuable input directly from the people who are involved in the process of creating or delivering products and services. Having their inputs will enable you to assess what other aspects of your business need improving and you can maintain the level of your business' performance.

Value of Feedback

If you want a substantial feedback, then you can get it directly from the people who avail of your products and services – the customers. As them for feedbacks on your brand to determine whether you are delivering the quality of standards you have set and they expect from you. If there are any dissatisfied customers, ask them for feedback on how you can improve the quality of your product or service. Your customer is probably your best source of honest criticism and should also provide you with a concrete idea on where you must improve.

Reviewing Your Brand

Successful brands are those that remain consistent with the needs of its consumers. Therefore, it is your duty to constantly review your brand and its performance to know whether you are meeting these standards. As times evolve, the needs of your customer changes as well. In fact, your customer base might change because of that. So, you need to adjust your branding strategy in accordance with changes in market demands and needs.

Even the most established brands change their marketing approach and branding strategy to stay attuned to the changing business trends in the market. Reviewing your brand must be something that you need to perform periodically; hence, you are always aware of any ongoing trends.

Importance of Reviewing Business Brand

The reviewing process involved in your business' branding strategy offer several beneficial opportunities for your business and its expansion. Here are just some of them:

• It is a good indicator of areas in the business that you can improve on or potentially expand.

• Be careful when trying to stretch or expand your products because it might end up similar to some other existing products. Better yet, reconsider the possibility of creating a new product instead.

• It will provide an avenue for more inputs and suggestions from inside or outside of your institution.

• It enables you to validate your company's core values and how your products or services remain consistent with that.

• Periodical assessment of your business brand enables you to keep up with changing business trends and market demands.

Useful Links

Top Five Books on Branding
http://marketing.about.com/od/brandstrategy/tp/top5
branding.htm


Brand Maker News
http://brandmakernews.com/personal-
brand/539/the-personal-brand-book-list-8-brand-
building-books-to-help-plot-your-takeover.html

Best Branding Books
http://www.how-to-branding.com/Best-Branding-
Books.html

# THE EXPERT GUIDE
## TO
# CYBER SECURITY

## BY
# WARREN BROWN

# INTRODUCTION

Dear Reader,

This book will help you to understand
Cybersecurity. It will be a guide for you in realizing
the importance of Cybersecurity in your life.


Sincerely
Warren Brown

London
2012

## What is Cybersecurity?

Every important transaction could be coursed online these days. You could shop across different Websites, do banking transactions, transfer money, pay electronically, and do just about anything. The importance of the Internet has become more concrete and more obvious. Many personal data are now stored and retrieved online. You could get access through your computer or though someone's system. Thus, cybersecurity is very significant.

Cybersecurity involves protection of sensitive personal and business information through prevention, detection, and response to different online attacks. As mentioned, because most important transactions are conducted across the Internet these days, there is a need to impose effective protection and measures to counter and repel cybercrimes, especially fraud.

You have probably heard of news stories about many credit card users who complain of overcharging because hackers use their accounts online. There are also different types of destructive email viruses that are not just aimed at destroying files, but also at hacking personal security codes and information like passwords. If you have been a victim of such cyber-crimes, you surely would understand the necessity for stronger cybersecurity measures.

The best defense against cyber-crimes is to understand risks and basic terms. You should also know about certain measures to achieve protection against cyber piracy and crimes. Cybersecurity is not a simple concept. It could get complicated because its scope is constantly and is aggressively expanding.

So what are the identified risks of cyber-crimes? Many risks are more serious and pressing than the others. Email viruses could erase your entire computer system without you knowing it. There are even viruses that are designed to break into computer systems to alter files and to further spread the reach of destruction. Some malicious software are made to steal credit card information of private individuals and make unauthorized purchases. As an active Internet user, there is definitely no guarantee that you would be fully exempted from experiencing such problems. But you could always take measures to minimize chances.

The first effective step to protect yourself from cyber-crimes and proliferation of computer viruses is to identify cyber criminals. Hackers, intruders, and attackers are people who seek to principally exploit weaknesses of computer systems and software for their own advantage. Their actions are always violating intended usage of computer systems. Many of them are motivated by curiosity, but still violations are punishable whatever the scale. Results of hacking and intruding activities could range from malicious to mere mischief consequences.

Malicious codes (also called malware) include codes that are used to attack any computer system. They come in various forms. Some are guised as email attachments, while others claim to do other activities. More dangerously, some malwares are contracted without the computer user's knowledge. Propagation of such malicious codes is getting more and more rampant these days. Classic and popular examples of malwares or malicious codes are worms and viruses.

Vulnerability is one issue computer users should always confront. In most cases, it is caused by software's programming errors. When such errors happen, attackers get the chance to infect your computer system. Thus, cybersecurity measures and programs should be installed and used to provide effective protection. You should always aim to protect yourself from online and computer attacks.

There are now many options that could help you address vulnerabilities.

# Why Do We Need Cyber Security?

Why do we need cyber security? There a number of reasons. The cyber community changes in an unbelievable pace. Unfortunately, along with these changes are equally unbelievable threats. The nature of the Internet as a tool for communication and education has been used and misused for personal gain, which resulted in cyber attacks and unprecedented rise in cyber crime rates. These rates are expected to increase more rapidly in the coming years if cyber security is not put in place. So, why exactly do we need cyber security? Let us count the reasons.

1.) Hackers are everywhere. He can be your business rival, your neighbor, or simply a person out to take over your computer. He makes use of software loopholes and hijacks your computer through backdoors, usually installed programs, or through cracking software. When he finally marches into your computer, he can gain access to possibly all your personal and confidential information such as bank accounts, credit cards, or top trade secret. He can also use your computer to attack other networks, with you apparently oblivious to all his malicious operations.

2.) Internet scams and frauds are rampant. These include phishing, a very organized cyber crime, which deceives people into giving their banking details. Cyber criminals, pretending to be representatives from legitimate financial institutions, send e-mail messages and ask unsuspecting people to verify their passwords, account numbers, and other vital information. According to a report, in 2006 alone, phishing attempts increased by 81%. These attempts could effectively be counterattacked if they weren't too sophisticated to actually deaden spam filters.

3.) Cyber theft is a common cyber crime. In fact, it is the most reported. Over time, it has increasingly become so easy for cyber criminals to steal information from computers, not only from individuals but for companies, banks, and other organizations as well. Though they hardly report the case, big companies lose large amounts of money.

4.) Virus can slow down your computer. Worse, it can cause system crash. Virus reaches your system through a number of entryways. One is through unsecured and unknown websites from which you download files, programs, applications, or tools for free. As much as it can infect home computers, virus can leave damaging effects to companies, both big and small. For instance, Melissa virus hit Microsoft and other big companies in 1999, which led them to temporarily terminate their e-mail systems.

5.) Spyware, as the name hints, can spy on you. A computer program automatically installed on your computer, spyware tracks personal information you entered and sends it to its creator. In most cases, spyware is used to steal big sum of money. Unlike computer viruses, spyware leaves the computer owners totally unaware of its presence. A study revealed that 92% of users with infected systems don't know that spyware has broken into their computers.

6.) Adware can keep unwanted ads to show up. Like spyware, adware penetrates the system through shareware. On its own, it downloads ads and allows them to run and pop up. This proves to be quite annoying for computer owners. But what's even more troubling is that adware can sometimes contain spyware. This increases the risk for cyber threats.

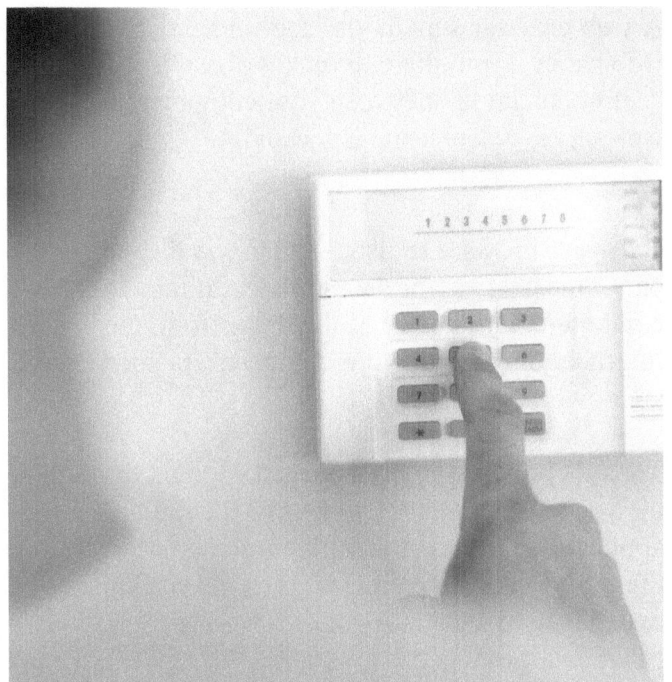

Why do we need cyber security? Cyber criminals are smart beings. They find ways to get into our systems and create havoc in less time than we expect. And because they don't cease to innovate and produce more sophisticated threats, we should always put our guard on and reinforce whatever cyber security measures we have these days.

**Your Browser – Cyber Security's 1st Line of Defense**

Nowadays, many people seemed to have forgotten the importance (and the inherent dangers) of their computer's browser. They forgot that the browser, per se, works like a two-way street. It is where cyber security should police the two-way cyber traffic.

A web browser's main job is to find and display web pages. From there, it makes possible the "communication" between your computer and the web server where a site is located.

Cyber security risks
But, your browser is also – and this is the dangerous part – the gateway of the cyber world into your computer. And, not all of the things from the Internet going inside your computer are good. Some are downright risky.

Today's browser is sophisticated enough, through the years of innovation, to handle the multiple applications needed to surf the Internet. Many of these try to boost up and heighten the surfing experience by enabling your browser's functionalities.

But sometimes, these functionalities are not needed and they can leave your computer vulnerable. It is therefore safe to disable them until they are needed.

In a perfect world, one should set one's browser security to the highest level possible. But these settings may restrict the functionality of other features and prevents some web pages to load properly. The best compromise solution would be to set your browser to the highest security level (to prevent attacks) but at the same time enabling some features to work when you need them.

Today's many browsers are mostly graphical browsers (Internet Explorer, Firefox, AOL, Opera, Safari for the Macintosh, and Lynx for the visually-impaired users.) These are capable of playing video and audio clips, aside from displaying texts and graphics. Most have user-friendly tabs and options in choosing your preferred security level setting.

It is important to know and be familiar with your browser and how it is different from the others. It will come in handy when you evaluate and determine the features and setting most appropriate for your use.

For instance, to explore the basic security options in Windows' Internet Explorer, you click Tools on the menu bar, select Internet Options, choose the Security tab, and click the Custom level. In Firefox, you click Tools first, select Options, and then click Content Privacy and Security tabs. The others have their own path systems.

Choosing your browser
Security should be paramount in choosing your browser. But, of course, given one's particular needs in surfing and using the Internet, other considerations are just as important. Sometimes, a browser comes packaged with the operating system. It should not limit, however, your choice.

Compatibility – does your browser work with the OS (operating system) of your computer?

Ease – are you comfortable and familiar with the options, menus, system of your browser?

Function –will it still work if other plug-ins or other devices are installed?

Appeal – do you like how your browser looks and works?

Functionalities - Your browser should be able to give you the option of putting web sites into different segments, or zones, and define different security restrictions for each. The best protection should be to set the security to the highest level, or maintain it at a medium level.

If you know of some sites which can be classified as trusted, you can set your browser setting accordingly. You may require them to implement SSL or Secure Sockets Layer so you can verify if they are what they claim to be. Note, however, that it is good to avoid lowering your security levels with them. If they are attacked, you might be included.

You may restrict particular sites you are not sure of. Prevention is always the best cure for any disease, real-life or online.

Be careful about your Java and ActiveX controls. These scripts, used to achieve certain appearances or functionality, can be used in attacking your computer. This is also true about Plug-ins, those additional software that enhances the function of some programs. Make sure that the sites that installing them are trustworthy.

For safety, it is advisable to disable Cookies and enable them only if the site you trust requires them.

Cyber Security starts first in your browser. It is best that you start the safeguarding process from there, your computer's door to the wide, wild world of cyber space.

Cyber Security and Identity Theft

Today's biggest cyber security concern is Identity Theft. Cyber thieves use all kinds of methods (hacking, use of spyware for intercepting information, etc.) in stealing personal or financial information from their victims, mostly from the computers.

The latest of these nefarious activities even sports a name: phishing (pronounced like "fishing"). The thief sends a simple e-mail that looks like it came from a genuine site (mostly from financial institutions as Citibank, eBay, PayPal, Best Buy and others), telling you there is a problem with your account.

They would then ask you to click on a certain link in the e-mail, and you are taken to a site that looks exactly like that of your bank. Here, they will ask you to fill out again your Social Security or credit card numbers, and/or other confidential numbers.

The following are some ways to minimize the risk of your identity being stolen:

Do business with reputable companies
Some attackers may try to trick you by creating web sites that appear to be legitimate.
Don't visit any site that is using third party links.
Open a new browser and type the address yourself if you want to visit a site.

You can also check privacy policies to see how the company in question use and distribute information. Many companies allow customers to request that their information not be shared with other companies.

Maintain a security mindset – always be skeptical of unfamiliar sites and links, suspicious e-mails and IM messages.

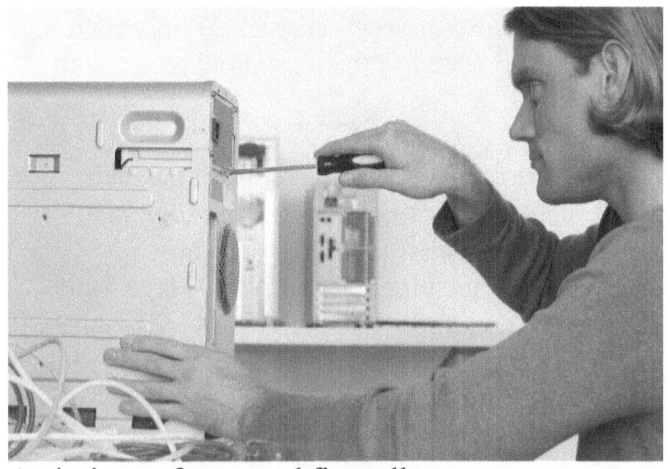

Anti-virus software and firewall
As standard practice, use and maintenance of an anti-virus software and firewall will protect your computer from attacks that may steal or modify data in your computer.
Make sure to keep your anti-virus program and firewall up to date.

Fighting identity robbery
As precautionary steps, regularly check your credit reports for strange transactions or transactions you don't recall, unusual charges on your bills, bills for products and services you don't have, or worse, unexpected denial of your credit card.

Once the identity robbery has been confirmed, calls to appropriate companies and agencies have to be done immediately. Have your credit card accounts closed right away so future charges will be denied.

Contact the Social Security Administration if your SSS card number has been accessed or the DMV if your driver's license or car registration papers were stolen. This is to warn these agencies for possible unauthorized use of your personal ID information. Of course, you need to file a criminal report with the local police.

For U.S. citizens, you need to contact the main credit reporting companies (Equifax, Experian, TransUnion) to see if there had been any unexpected or unauthorized activity. Have fraud alerts placed on your credit reports to prevent new accounts from being opened without verification. File a complaint with the FTC and IFCC.

A website, IdentityTheftActionPlan.com, had been created to help citizens prevent, detect, and respond to identity theft and fraud. Within the site is information on how identity theft occurs, the latest prevention tips, what to do in case you are victimized and pertinent information of law enforcement agencies that investigate these crimes. Two other sites to learn more about phishing and ID theft are the following: consumer.gov/idtheft/ and idtheftcenter.org

Vigilance, information and action
Cyber security dictates that every cyber citizen (those using computers and the Internet in most of their activities) needs to be vigilant at all times.

Everyone is enjoined to keep up with the latest information, so that they can do the appropriate action by themselves.

Cyber Security and Online Shopping

With the popularity of online shopping today, the importance of cyber security becomes essential to everyone. Shopping, even in the real world, involves money and where there is money, there go the criminals. And since much shopping is now happening in cyber space, these criminals lost no time in following the money trail targeting online shoppers.

Online shopping became fashionable when people discovered one is free from stress and fatigue caused by crowds and traffic. There is also the convenience of searching whatever it is you want from your home, at your most convenient time, and paying for it without waiting in line. All of these with just a few click of a mouse.

However, the Internet is also a convenient place for cyber criminals as well. They target the online shoppers, fraudulently obtaining information they can use for their own financial gains. These criminals use the three most common ways in attacking the online shoppers.

Unprotected computers
Unprotected computers are easy target for viruses and other malicious codes used by cyber criminals to gain access to the information inside it. On the other end, online vendors have to protect their computers, too, against attackers who may access their customer databases.

Fake sites and email messages
In the virtual online world, a site (or an online store) can be faked by these criminals, with no one the wiser. These fake sites mimic the legitimate ones and inherit the business, at least until they are caught or noticed.

Charities had been misrepresented before, especially during natural disasters or holiday seasons where people pour in donation money and aid. Most often, though, these attackers collect information for their own illegal use.

Cyber safety measures
Maintaining an up-to-date anti-virus program, a firewall and anti-spyware is always the three-pronged first line of defense in cyber security. They protect you against viruses and Trojan horses that

may steal or modify your data and make your computer vulnerable. Spyware may also give the attackers access to your data.

Updated browser
Browsers are the gateway between your computer and the Internet. They must be updated first. Also, open the option of automatic updates to your computer so that the operating programs and utilities are up to date.

It is likewise important to check the default settings of your computer and apply the highest level of security. This will preempt the attackers to use default setting of the programs. This applies primarily to browsers, email clients, etc. because these are the connectors to the Internet.

Reputable vendors
This is where care should be taken because cyber criminals are very good at mimicking the sites of legitimate vendors and make it appear genuine. You need to verify their legitimacy before supplying any information. Keep the phone numbers and the physical addresses of these vendors which you can use in case of problems.

Security features and private policies
As always, passwords and other security features add protection, if correctly used. Check the site's privacy policy before giving out personal or financial information. You have to understand how your information are stored and used.

Encrypted information
Make sure the information you give out are
encrypted. To check if it is, see if it includes a URL
that begins with "https:" instead of "http:" and a
padlock icon. If the padlock is closed, the
information is encrypted. Know where the padlock
icon is located in your favorite browser because
some attackers use fake padlock icons to trick users.

Use your credit card
Credit card charges have laws that limit your
liability in case of fraud. This may not be the case
for your debit card. Because debit cards draw
money directly from your bank account,
unauthorized withdrawals could leave you
penniless. Needless to say, a record of your
purchases should be kept aside. Report immediately
any discrepancy.

Shopping online is truly a time-saving, hassle-free,
and fun way of buying whatever you want on the
Internet. The presence of the ubiquitous cyber
criminals stalking at every cyber corner necessitates
the need of cyber security as well.

It is everyone's responsibility.

Cyber Security Building a Good Habit

Cyber security is not at all that difficult. Once you have incorporated it into your system then it is just like riding a bicycle or can be as normal as walking. All you need is to learn how you can make it work well and build a good habit to make cyber security consistent.

By doing this you can have a better chance of keeping your confidential information protected from attacks from virus or similar applications or from hackers. This way you can keep your personal information safe from other persons who would like to access them and use them for personal gain or protect them from applications that can erase or corrupt your files.

Part of building a good habit would be to identify how your information can be accessed and who would be the most likely people who can gain from accessing your confidential files. It's like identifying the usual suspects in a criminal line-up. I'm not saying that the people you know cannot be trusted but it helps to be extra cautious. You brother might not do something untrustworthy by his friends might and if they have physical access to your computer then your files are at a risk of being hacked.

Lock your computer with a good password. Use combinations of letters and numbers, upper case and lower case, and even use codes. Avoid using the usual birthdays, social security numbers, bank PINs, account numbers, favourite superheroes, favourite food, etc. Use unique passwords and make one up for every system that requires authentication. Do not use the same password in all your confidential files.

To protect your computer from outside hackers, the best thing would be to disconnect your computer from the network when you're not using it. No anti-virus application or firewall systems provide 100 per cent protection. The best way would be to remove yourself from the network when you're not using your computer to reduce the risk of being attacked.

When you do go online, make sure that you have your firewall on and your anti-virus application active. Also look into your security settings. Your emails, web browsers and even other applications have specific settings which increase the security allowing them to block attacks from virus, malware and spyware. Study the security settings and select one which permits you to maximize the use of the application but at the same time offer you a good deal of security to keep your files protected.

Also, do not forget about power surges and other technological problems. Even though, the virus and hacker threats are real and sometimes the priority, people also forget that sometimes power surges or breakdown of computer hardware can cause loss of data or have files corrupted and rendered unusable.

To have added protection therefore, it would be wise to install some uninterrupted power supply that protects your from power surges and allows you to back up or shut down your computer properly preventing possible corruption of files and applications.

And speaking of backing up, it would be great if you would regularly back up your files just in case the unthinkable happens. May these be personal files or files you need for work, having a good back up is always a good thing to have.

You see, once you have a system you will develop a good habit in cyber security which can help reduce the risks of losing files or your confidential information being hacked.

Cyber Security for Kids

If you think your kids now just need to be protected
from strangers offering them candy or from cars
while crossing the streets, then you have another
thing coming. Your children need a whole new level
of protection especially in this age of computers and
the internet. More and more kids are having easier
access to the internet. According to some studies,
more than 80% of teenagers in the US have access
to the internet at home. The parents should take an
active role in teaching their children proper cyber
security measures.

Most of the time these kids who access the net are
not careful enough when giving out personal
information online. They don't realize yet the risks
of not having confidential and personal information
protected online. From virus, to hackers, to identity
thieves, these people are lurking in cyberspace
waiting for that opportunity. I can only stress the
importance of cyber security for kids.

Now there are several ways where you can help
instill to your children the proper ways of accessing,
behaving and protecting themselves online. One of
the more common venue where your children go on
the web is the social network sites where they have
online profiles, photos and keep blogs or online
journals. Remind your kids that not to accept all
those you invite them to be their online friend
especially if they don't know that person.

The problem with these social network sites is that
once you add someone as a friend, you can be
viewed by friends included in his own network

which most of time you don't even know. These are venues where scrupulous individuals can gain access to your personals.

To monitor their browsing activities or encourage them to ask questions, place your computer in an area of the house where there's heavy foot traffic. This will make it easy for them to call your attention to their monitor if they want to ask questions or show you something. This also discourages them from visiting lewd and pornographic websites.

These websites are not only inappropriate but are also a repository of malware, spyware and virus applications that can destroy files and even your whole computer system. In this regard, it would be best to use controlling mechanisms like content blockers which prohibits them to access certain websites and also monitoring application so you can take a look later what they actually look for in the net.

It is always good to engage your children in a healthy conversation about the things that did or things they can do online. This way you can teach them proper ways or help develop good habits that will ensure their safety online. You can also teach them the pros and cons of social networking, online file sharing, and even the issues of software piracy and illegal downloads. These are part of increasing their knowledge and understanding about the technology of computers and the net as well as cyber security.

You should always remember that children's predisposition of being still curious, innocent, and sometimes their desire to be independent can cause them to be careless. That is why ordinary safeguards are not enough when it comes to protection your kids on cyberspace. The previously mentioned cyber security measures for kids are not just an introduction.

You will have to know for a fact your kids computer habits and then learn how you can better protect them.

Cyber Security: Password Protected

You turn on your computer and you're prompt with a username and password. The same thing happens when you open your email account. I know it is quite obvious to you right now but allow me to stress the importance of cyber security by having password protected files, networks, and software applications. It is important to protect your personal information. Sure, it seems unimportant if people hacked into your email account.

You have a bunch of personal emails from friends and occasionally send some your self but the whole lot of your mails in your inbox are spam and other promotional garbage, so why do you have to care that much. But the thing is, those who are able to gain access to your email accounts are often not truly satisfied with that level of attach and are in reality just preparing for a much bigger intrusion.

Before you know it, they can get information about your social security number of even bank accounts. Your personal emails contain heaps of information which can be used by hackers for their own personal gain.

Having a good password installed is therefore a good deterrent for hackers or attackers. It ensures that proper authentication is verified first before you gain access to personal information. It is therefore important that you make up a good password. A poorly made one will just be ineffective and totally useless against hackers.

For instance, using part of your name as a password would be just too easy to crack. It will not be a deterrent at all. To add to this, there are applications like virus and worms that can actually penetrate a secure or confidential system just because it has a weak password installed.

Example of weak passwords, aside from a derivative from your name, would be using numbers that coincides with birthdays, phone numbers, addresses and information about your family or stuff. Sure, these are easy to remember but that thinking will also cause you problems later on. These kinds of numeric passwords are just easy to solve. The same thing goes with dictionary based passwords which are those words that you picked up from a dictionary.

Now in making up your password, it would be a lot better if you use combinations of letter, numbers and other techniques. You could intentionally misspell the words so you won't fall for dictionary attackers. You can add numbers and a combination of upper and lower cases. Or you could assign a code.

You can abbreviate something that if you love "watching soap shows on TV" you can take the first letters of the word "WsSoT" and combine it with a relevant numbers. Not only would the acronym easy to remember but it would be difficult for hackers to crack. However, avoid using famous quotes, catch phrases, lyrics, poem and even pick up lines. Go for something you invented.

Also, remember that having a longer password is better. The more characters you have the harder it is to guess or the more difficult to decipher the combinations. Also, don't use the same password twice for your other accounts. Although this is quite tempting since you don't have to create a new one and remember it every time, when an attacker does get a password from one of your accounts, the first thing he will do is to try the same password for all your other accounts.

Cyber security begins with you. Keeping your personal information safe lies first on password protected access to your files, systems and networks. Having a right and strong password will help fight off attackers.

# Cyber Security Regulations

Cyber security is meant to protect personal and work-related data and information stored in our computer and personal websites. With the increase of individuals, organizations, and members of the community falling prey to cyber crimes and security attacks, there is an increase in demands for more measures to be taken.

Alarmingly, the number of people getting affected cyber security attacks is increasing. According to a research by Panda Software in 2006, 1 out of 5 e-mail messages that corporate servers receive are spam and 1 out of 20 is infected with malware. Consumer Reports released a report in 2006 showing that United States consumers would spend $7.8 billion over the last two years for computer repairs and replacements because security attacks like malware and viruses.

Security attacks like these do not only costs an individual repairs, businesses, organizations and the national economy could suffer losses. In 2005, cyber crime led to a loss of whopping $130.1 million, all because of viruses, unauthorized access to computer systems and personal and financial information theft.

There are numerous measures that should be taken by the government to help resolve cyber crimes and attacks. In the United States, there are different legislations in the executive and Congress level that are meant to protect computer systems and other medium of information technology. This is called cyber-security regulations.

Cyber –security regulations is to make sure that companies and private institutions would be using or protecting their systems from any cyber attacks like viruses, worms, phishing, denial of service and unauthorized access.

The United States Chamber of Commerce said that there are about 64 % of small businesses that are getting protection for their systems to protect their customer's financial information.  While there are about 72 % of businesses expressed concern about security of the company's assets and information.

In the United States, there are cyber-security regulations, for both federal and estate governments.  For federal government cyber security regulations, they focus mainly on specific industries and fields, healthcare, organizations, financial institutions and agencies that work with systems and information.   Unfortunately, this regulation do not reach and cover computer related industries like Internet Service Providers (ISP).

Additional to this, the federal government is also trying to resolve issues of cyber security breach by allocating more funds in research and programs directed to research better solutions and recommendations for improving cyber security. The government is collaborating with members of the private sector.

Meanwhile, states are forming their own methods of dealing with security attacks.  An example is the regulation passed by the California State in 2003 called Notice of Security Breach Act.  Different states have followed the example of California and created their own anti-breach regulations and standard procedure.

There has been an on-going debate about cyber security regulation. There are people who comments that creating a regulation is not the answer and not enough, what is needed is better defenses against hackers, viruses and similar threats. The regulation is said to restrict industries to develop programs and software that would boost cyber security. Aside from this, businesses also fears that having the regulation will cut back their healthy profits since they would meet more limitations and would cost them more.

But inspite of regulations and software that could protect your computer and systems, still the best way to boost cyber security is preventing any attacks from happening in the first place. There are easy tips that could be followed to avoid cyber attacks from happening.

Cyber Security Threats

Cyber security is about protecting your computer from any threat that may use you data and information without authority, protect you machine from different threats like viruses, worms, spyware, and malware. When these threats are blended together, they can overload and shut down systems and resources.

Everybody seems to rely on computer nowadays, bill payments can be done online, communication, transportation, entertainment and other aspects of our lives depend or influenced by computers. This is why computer or cyber security threats are important to be dealt immediately.

There are different kinds of cyber security threats, for example, our browsers are not that safe anymore. Browsers have vulnerabilities where expert hackers can exploit codes and passwords. Hackers would use even our trusted websites to make these attacks. This is why software manufacturers are investing on security to setup tools that would protect users even on trusted sites.

Another alarming security threat is that there are an increased number of incidents where national records are extracted. Economic data of a nation or state can fall victims to cyber theft. National and state governments are not the only victims, in the United Kingdom cyber theft is recognized to be among the biggest crime in the country. Cyber theft could include credit card fraud, illegal bank transfers and phishing attacks.

Phishing attacks are fraudulent processes where sensitive personal and financial information are asked from an individual. People would fall victims to phishing scams since they pose as legal and trustworthy institutions, they are normally send out through emails and instant messaging.

Computers are not the only targets of cyber threats, mobile phones are also being attacked by worms, viruses, and malware. Mobile phones are very susceptible to hackers and also viruses. Old cellphones can be immune to viruses, but new cellphones, the smart ones, because of their standardized operating system are now in risk of viruses.

Multimedia messaging services or MMS can send multiple copies of the phone address book or copy the phone book into a new handset just within a couple of minutes. Aside from that it could also infect other phones within the area and disrupt communication protocols.

Cyber-terrorism is also another increasing cyber security threat experienced by users. Some experts would say that cyber terrorism is just the same as hacking. But experts would agree that it is intended to create or start fear, physical harm or death by using electronic methods.

An example would be the case in Romania, where terrorists were able to control the life support systems in an Antarctic research station, putting 58 scientists in danger. This kind of attack can affect a great deal of people, weaken the economy and even make the country vulnerable to military attacks.

Another common cyber security problem would be the attacks of people themselves, like disgruntled employees. In a survey conducted by the Nucleus Research and KnowledgeStorm, 1 out 3 workers would jot down their passwords. This is not the best security practice since jotted down passwords can be lost and used by unsatisfied workers.

There are increasing number of cyber security threats that needs to be addressed immediately. Long-term plans and solutions should be created to address the increasing number of victims. While we wait for government and organizations to come up with long-term solutions, it is our individual responsibility to make sure that we keep our personal and work-related information safe.

# Family Cyber Security

Keeping your family safe today takes on another additional front – online or the Net. The perils that you and your family face whenever anyone is online are just as dangerous as in real life. There simply is a need for cyber security to minimize, if not totally deflect, these dangers.

Cyber security is not just to protect you and your children from online dangers. It is also to ensure that your computer is safe and secure – from your children. By following some simple computer practices, these dangers can be lessened.

The usual safeguards may not be adequate. Children, by nature, are curious and inquisitive. They like to pry things, satisfy their natural need to know.

As parents, there is a delicate balance on how long the lease we give out to kids to satisfy their natural need and the necessity to protect themselves from the outside world and from themselves.

A child out into the Net, either playing a game, researching materials for homework or a term paper can be potentially harmed. Common accidents would be your child stumbling into a porn site, getting into malicious web pages that infect your computer, or inadvertently erasing your own computer's files.

Mistakes like these happen and your child may not be aware of them. Or if they are, they may not inform you what happened for fear of punishment.

Another fearsome threat is the 'online predator'. Because of the Internet's natural cover for anonymity, these people deceive and manipulate other online users to get what they want. Adults are common victims of these people, and it follows that children are even more susceptible to their dangerous manipulative schemes.

The following are some suggested safeguards in implementing cyber security in the family.

Be involved with your children's activities
There are some activities you can do with your kids that will in effect allow you to supervise their activities. If this is not possible, you can always monitor their computer use – which sites they visit, the activities they do online, etc. If they are using emails and chat rooms, try to follow who they are corresponding with, and whether they actually know them.

## Rules and danger warnings

The children should be made aware about online dangers. They must be able to recognize suspicious behaviour or activities from the Net.

This will help you set out boundaries on their computer use. Everything, of course, should be appropriate for their age, knowledge and level of maturity. It is not correct to scare them, but to make them be alert and aware. This includes sites they are allowed to visit, programs they can use, and activities they can do.

Separate accounts and other controls
Today's operating systems already carries the option of creating different user accounts on one computer. You can create separate accounts for them to protect your own files and data from accidentally accessed, modified, or – horrors! – deleted.

If you don't have separate accounts, consider limiting the functionality of your browser (like remembering passwords, other information, etc.) to preclude accidental access.
It is here that it is important to keep your anti-virus utility, firewalls, and other safeguards up to date and active.

Some browsers allow you to restrict viewing certain web sites and protect these settings with a password. (click Tools, select Internet Options, choose the Content tab, click Enable under Content Advisor, etc.)

Some service providers also offer services that protect children who go online. They can help filter and block sites that are not suited to children. The Internet is also full of special programs for children's protection. Check those that suits your needs best.

Open communications and computers
Set your computer in an open area of the house where everyone can monitor anyone's computer activities. It can deter children from doing things not allowed.

Most important, communication lines between all members of the family should be kept open. The children must know that they can approach their parents at any time about anything they see on the computer.

This is very important, not just for cyber security, but also for the family's well-being as a whole, whether anybody is online or not.

# Cyber Security Tips For Your Protection

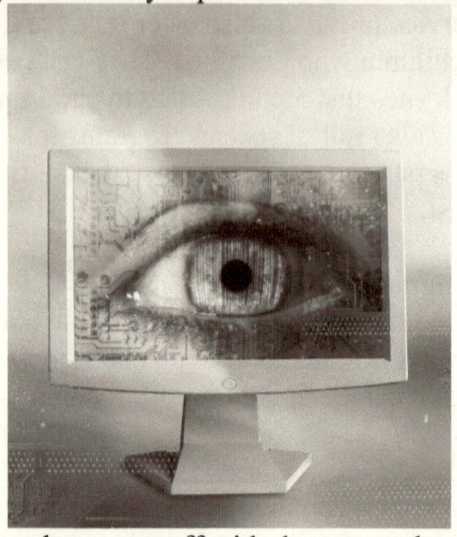

Many people are put off with the term cyber security. They think it involves highly technological processes and elaborate computer knowledge. Not at all. Cyber security is foremost about identifying threats and taking measures as simple as creating an indecipherable password. There is nothing too technical about that. In fact, cyber security measures are all too simple to follow. Check out the following cyber security tips.

1.) Use strong passwords. Avoid using names, birthdays, addresses, and other personal information as password. Do not use a word found in the dictionary as well, since hackers have found a way to decipher dictionary-generated passwords using certain tools. In general, a good password is at least eight-characters long and should be hard to crack. You can combine upper- and lower-case letters, numbers, and symbols. One good practice is to form a password from a phrase. For example, you can create t1$!C4gtMpSd from "This is so I can't forget my password." You can use other methods with which you can form unique and cryptic passwords.

2.) Change your password periodically. This is important especially if, at some point, you have to disclose your password. Remember not to write it down, or if you should, discard the paper immediately. You never know the danger negligence can impose on your security.

3.) Be scrupulous with emails. Unsolicited emails are sometimes the onset of cyber attacks. Remember not to open attached files from unknown senders, as they may contain malware that can open backdoors for hackers. Clicking on the links can also direct you to some compromising websites, so be cautious. If a link looks suspicious, look it up on the web and do a quick research. Avoid giving information to unknown senders as well. The rule of thumb is to ignore seemingly malicious mails. Do not reply to and forward them.

4.) Install security programs on your computer and keep them updated. It is very important to have anti-virus and anti-spyware software and to keep your firewall on. Poorly secured systems are open doors for attackers and intruders, but these software programs keep viruses and spyware from penetrating and crippling your system. The firewall, on the other hand, guards your system from unauthorized access to your computer. Some operating systems allow automatic security updates. Check if yours have this option.

5.) Avoid opening files sent through Instant Messenger. These files do not undergo scanning and might carry security threats to your computer.

6.) Ignore the links on pop-up windows. Block pop-up ads and windows to close an entryway for malware and other forms of attack.

7.) Avoid downloading files, programs, applications, or tools from unknown websites. More often than not, these free downloadable stuffs are loaded with threats. Before you download, make sure the website is a credible source.

8.) Make sure to keep your system clean. Remove any tool, application, or program that is not used. Check also unused default programs installed on your operating system. It's better to have few programs than have many but unused ones, which can only slow down your computer and be an opening for malicious attacks.

A poorly secured computer runs the risk of being hijacked and left as a zombie machine. Secretly, the hacker uses this computer to gain access to personal and confidential accounts and information. Next thing you know, your credit card has been used for unauthorized purchases, your savings account has been ransacked, your competitor has spied on your company, and the list can go on and on.

But some simple and easy-to-follow cyber security tips can eliminate the possibility of falling prey to any of these cyber crimes.

# More Cyber Security Tips

In today's digital age, cyber security is as important, if not more so, as actual security guarding a real piece of company property. However they may differ, they both have safeguard strategies that need to be implemented to the letter to be effective.

The following are some guidelines for use in cyber security:

Up-to-date anti-virus software
This is a given: all computers must have anti-virus software. The anti-virus software is specifically created and designed to protect your computer against known viruses.

There is one caveat, however. New viruses are created almost daily. There is a need, therefore, to update your anti-virus program on a regular basis to recognize these new variants of viruses.

Like flu shots, only that they are done more often, these regular updates can help stop these viruses. These regular updates are antidotes for these man-made vermin.

Firewalls
Firewalls are virtual defensive fortifications to protect your computer from the outside world. They filter unauthorized data from elsewhere, mostly the Internet, while allowing authorized or 'good' data to enter your computer.

All types of firewalls are available in most computer stores, and some computer manufacturing companies bundle them together with their computers that you purchase.

Emails

The simplest rule is this: if you don't know the person who is sending you an email, be very careful about opening the email and never open any file attached to it.

Sometimes, you may have a vague idea who the sender is, but you should still be careful.
Some tell-tale signs include unusual hyperlinks and/or urgent messages to open the attached file.
Some of your friends may have been conned and unwittingly forwarded you a virus-laden email.

When in doubt, delete. Your friend will understand.

Passwords

Passwords were created to be your virtual key to computer data. Like real-life keys, passwords are only as good if they are difficult to 'duplicate' or guessed.

Some of the guidelines are: Don't share your password, don't use your same password in more than one place, and most importantly, create a password that is difficult to guess.
Here are some time-tested rules in password-making:

1.) Passwords should have a minimum of 8 characters, and should be as meaningless as possible.

2.) Use all kinds of types possible – lower case, upper case, numbers, symbols, special characters, etc.

3.) Change your passwords regularly, every three months, for example.

4.) Never give out your password to anybody.

Back-up Data

Experienced computer users know one primary rule: always back up your data. Small amounts of data can be stored on disks and on CDs if they are more than the disk can handle. For computers in a network, the usual backup is through the network data storage system. The overall idea is that if anything happens to your primary data, you can always retrieve them from somewhere.

File sharing
Another big no-no for experienced computer users is sharing them with strangers. Your computer operating system may allow file sharing from other computers in your network or from the Internet. This is one sure way of infecting your computer. Be

sure to turn off and disable file-sharing if it is not needed.

Disconnecting from the Internet
Cutting your computer's connection with the Internet when not in use lessens the possibility of accessing it. If your computer has no firewall or updated anti-virus protection, someone could harm it.

Update security patches
Just like your anti-virus program, there is a need to regularly update your other computer programs. Sometimes, bugs are discovered in your regular programs that can be an entrance to your computer for any malicious person to attack and infect.

Software companies create patches for these and post them in their sites. They can be downloaded and are automatically patched up into your program in question.

Regular security checkups
Like a car's multiple systems, a computer security programs need regular checkups, too. Sometimes, you may discover that a program is outdated through simple oversight. Some security settings have to be adjusted according to your present needs. Twice-a-year evaluation is good enough.

Security awareness
Like preparing for emergencies in real life, it is good policy to make sure that family members or probably your employees would know what to do during computer emergencies.

They must at least be aware of proper computer security practices – how to update virus protection programs, how to download patches, how to create proper passwords.

Cyber security, like any real security, needs everybody's help for it to succeed and avert those dreaded computer attacks.

# Facing Computer And Cyber Security Threats

Who did fall for any cyber security threat? Cyber security crimes are not just limited to hacking, financial, personal and work-related information theft. Viruses, worms, Trojan horse, spyware and malware are among the cyber security threats that can affect our computers and machines and our personal lives as well.

Consumer Reports reported in 2006 that U.S. consumers would spend $7.8 billion in the last two years for computer repairs, parts and replacements because of being attacked by malware and viruses. Everybody is being concerned with cyber attacks, businesses whether they are major or small businesses are expressing concern about the increasing ability of security threats to infiltrate information. Businesses are taking necessary steps to protect their customer's financial information.

The government can also be exposed to cyber security threats. Allowing public access can also increase the risks of data leaks, infiltration and cyber attacks. Therefore it is necessary to invest and have intensive and long-term solutions that would address cyber attacks.

Government agencies are coming up with methods that could help in addressing cyber attacks. Aside from these programs, as individuals or organizations, there are also ways to help in providing with long-term solutions to quick-developing problems. Here are some steps that the government has taken so far.

• There are different kinds of agencies and institutions dedicated in fighting cyber attacks. InfraGard is actually a partnership between the FBI and different members of the private sector like businesses , academic institutions, state and local law enforcement agencies and individuals. These 30,000 strong-organization is dedicated in sharing different kinds of information and intelligence to address criminal and violent acts.

• The government and also different organizations are reaching out to more CEOs of different businesses to help them understand cyber threat and what is needed to be done. This would help the government to come up with resources and policies that would help them build long- term prevention plans.

• Aside from local and national partnerships, international partnerships are also being done. Cyber security is not just an issue of one country, it is a global issue. Data and numbers of cyber security victims have encompasses geographical location and race. Cyber security issues can never be resolved by one nation alone. This would require coordination among countries at regional and global levels.

• Analyze and evaluate the loopholes and vulnerabilities. Agencies and institutions who have major cyber security problems, normally have networks and users spread out in different buildings and networks. Avoiding any cyber security problems and threat would be about identifying vulnerabilities and overcoming this.

• When looking for solutions, the you would have to stick to the basics. Technology is a dynamic process, it is a continuous change and improvement. The only way to make sure that your infrastructure and your system is safe is being prepared for it.

Cyber security threats do not stay the same over a period of time. It evolves. It changes and could go around the different security barriers set up to face its attacks.

How many times have we heard that the best cure is prevention? We should be thinking about that. Too much reliance and putting too much of our lives on computers has a risk that we should be able to handle and face. We should be prepared in hading cyber security issues from case to case and in every moment.

# Cyber Security Training: Tips And Guides

Despite the economic turmoil, reports said that cyber security professionals take home relatively high pay. It appears that companies see the benefit of investing in information and data security. While this can't drive business expansion, it can at the very least protect their businesses from further downhill glide and help them get by until the economy rises back to life.

This only proves that a cyber security career is not only lucrative but also timely. But you don't become a certified cyber security professional that easy; knowledge of computer and technology is not enough. You have to undergo cyber security training.

But how do you start? What's the first step? Start by looking for potential training school. Fortunately, many schools join the hype in cyber security and offer certificate and degree programs. Gather as much information as you can, then start comparing. As much as possible, avoid enrolling in online schools. Potential companies need to see evidence of your actual training, and online training can hardly give them that. Learning from books is good as well, but again, you need to build your expertise under the mentorship of physical teachers who can guide you through the ropes of security jobs in an interactive setting.

Of course, you will find that some schools are more expensive than the others. Take note, however, that costs are highly based on the mentors' expertise, laboratories, and facilities. If you find a school rather expensive, check if the teachers are experienced practitioners and do not merely echo what is written in the book. Remember, this is a skill training, and impartation of skills is necessary here.

Make sure as well that the laboratories and classrooms are well equipped, the machines and equipment modern, and the training location highly conducive to learning. Higher price translates to better service; this is the general rule.

After considering everything, here comes the hard part—actual learning. The best schools, teachers, and equipment are all secondary; the most important thing is your eagerness and dedication to learn. Make extra effort to supplement your training with research and consistent practices. If you need to setup a network at home to further study and employ what you've learn from your training, do so.

You sure will encounter errors and problems along the way, but these encounters are often good opportunities for learning. Research as much as you can. Get good books. The idea here is to learn more by immersing yourself in real-life scenarios.

You can also do volunteer work for small-scale businesses or non-profit organizations. There is a two-fold benefit to doing this. First, you can gain experience in a more professional setting. Second, these organizations are credible references in your future job application.

After passing your training, get active in looking for potential employment. But don't get frustrated if you don't immediately get into your dream company. Sometimes companies bank on years of experience, so to take this as an opportunity to gather more working experience. Start by offering your services to companies within your area.

Do not stop learning. Cyber security training is just the start. After this, you are on your own to feed your mind and hone your skill. Attend conferences if the opportunity arises. Consistently meet with other security professionals.

This way, not only will you be learning, you can also meet a lot of people who will either be willing to work with you or offer you employment opportunities.

# Further Equipping Cybersecurity Professionals

Cybersecurity is becoming a more important issue and aspect of information technology these days. The virtual world is getting bigger and bigger. Everyday, there are hundreds to thousands of new Websites that are made, complementing about millions of new Internet users across the globe. Different types of cyber crimes and security issues also abound.

There is a growing call for cybersecurity education to be further revamped. Many professionals, Internet users, legislators, and IT experts are calling for diversity in cybersecurity education and training. Professionals in the field should be trained and educated not only in the specific technology but also in other related subjects like business strategies, ethics, human relations, and law. To some proponents of this initiative, cybersecurity professionals should function more like renaissance men and women who are geared to meeting modern day challenges.

There is a growing call for developing a new and more skilled breed of multidisciplinary experts in the online security. Many education and IT experts are also asking diversity into psychology and organizational behaviour. There is a need to understand that online security practitioners are practically trained instead of educated. Current trainings for cybersecurity professionals include use of certain applications, techniques, and tools.

There is no specific course that helps professionals gain better and useful understanding of behaviours and principles that make up Internet security. Thus, diversification of training to transform as formal education is endorsed by many.

It is also highlighted that currently, there are only a few universities and institutions that offer cybersecurity programs for would-be Internet professionals. Aside from making cybersecurity a formal education, many people are also calling for the subject to be a full-length profession. This underlines the importance and necessity of online security.

Some IT experts are already envisioning a professional degree in cybersecurity that covers specific technical subjects like distributed systems, computer security principles, networking, software engineering, systems reliability, cryptography, and use of human factors and interfaces. Of course, mentioned specific multi-disciplinary subjects are also proposed to be included.

There are also calls to make trainings and education for cybersecurity a multidisciplinary undergraduate program in college. This is to institute and enhance professionals' system trustworthiness, which should be the foundation of IT professionals majoring in Internet security. Proponents like cybersecurity courses to be analogous to pre-med and pre-law courses in tertiary education. Several courses should be offered from different academic departments.

The goal of broadening cybersecurity education is to facilitate usage of every conceivable policy and technical tools for achievement of trustworthiness. Doing so is also believed to ensure that IT solutions would be eventually evaluated in broader societal contexts. This is for the purpose of contemplating trade-offs and risk management between varied social values like privacy versus accountability.

Of course, it is just obvious that Internet security has become a really important issue these days. As almost all businesses move only and basic business transactions get completed and coursed through the Internet, ensuring overall security is very important. Cybersecurity should be addressed more. Professionals of course need to be further equipped with necessary education way beyond training for technical skills. The Internet is fast and is constantly expanding. So do online security problems and issues.

It is better to improve current systems and further equip professionals than to be sorry in the future.

Know the Truth, Exposing Myths in Cyber Security

We all know the cyber security is important. Having a good password is important to keep confidential information protected. We know that having an anti-virus, anti-malware and spyware application do wonders especially when you're connected into a network or the web. Having all those applications is a good thing but we also know that having a correct firewall setting is quite important as well.

However, what most of us don't know and what we are forced to believe is that having these precautionary measures are just enough. Well they are not. It is time that you know the truth and expose some of the myths cyber security that we have believed for years.

Let's start of with anti-virus software and your system firewall. Despite what manufacturers say, despite what the advertisements say, despite what some of your friends tell you, no anti-virus software or firewalls for that matter are 100% effective. You need to understand that for one virus creators make malicious codes that are so advanced that an anti-virus application is not yet capable of handling an attack from it.

Despite the regular updates released by anti-virus software companies, they cannot foresee what kinds of virus will come out next month or the month after that. They can only provide their customers with protection based on the virus that they know off and the potential virus that could come out. As mentioned or implied earlier, the best way to have a degree of protection is combine the technologies together. Have separate virus software installed and keep a strong firewall active. Although, there might be a problem with some applications not working well together but conduct your won research and see which software works well together.

It is also important to know that not because you have installed an application that's the end of it. You see you will need to get the patches or updates that manufacturers release. These patches or updates are fixes on some little or sometimes big inconsistencies or bugs in the application. This is very important for anti-virus applications especially.

Look into your installed application and see it there is a n automatic updating option, which there usually is, that allows you to automatically receive updates whenever manufacturers release a new version or an upgrade of the system.

Also, don't believe that just because you have mainly personal and insignificant information in your computer that it's not worth protecting at all. Please bear in mind that what you think is not important can turn out be quite useful for hackers. Every bit of information you have in your computer, email or any other system can be manipulated and used by hackers to access more of your confidential information or use it to gain some profit. Even if you keep your files in a computer not connected to any network, the one that a hacker gains access to can be used to attack other computers or cause problems with other systems.

Not being rich is not a good enough reason of being attacked as well. Hackers and identity thieves will grab any opportunity that they come across with. If they can get you personal information easily, they will do so and think about how they can use it for their personal gain and believe me, they will think of a way.

After we exposed some of these myths and now you know the truth cyber security, I hope you get a renewed conviction regarding cyber security.


## More Governments Acquire Awareness in Cybersecurity Challenges


As the issues about cybersecurity become one of the most pressing concerns of US President Obama, other national governments are acting without hesitation to find solutions to current and future Internet security problems. This is not surprising given the fact that cybersecurity fever spreads like wildfire globally.

Experts aggressively warn that if appropriate Internet security measures are not conducted to provide protection to sensitive information across the virtual world, vulnerabilities in cybersecurity could seriously pose threats to overall security of nations, not just individuals and companies. This makes the subject all the more interesting and necessary.

African and Arab countries are joining hand in hand to achieve cybersecurity measures. In the middle of

2009, the Tunisian International Telecommunication Union or ITU organized a Regional Cybersecurity Forum. The event was attended by IT representatives from Africa and Middle Eastern Arab countries, as mentioned. It was dubbed as 'Connecting World Responsibility.'

The major task of the forum was for identification of several challenges that global nations face to be able to enhance cybersecurity and at the same time secure the right infrastructure for protection of critical data. The forum is aimed at assessing participating countries' measures in confronting cybercrime threats. Such evaluations are important given the fact that currently, advanced information and communications technologies are giving pirates more opportunities to exploit the Internet to commit cybercrimes and defraud more individuals and businesses.

IT experts and cybersecurity professionals should recognize the fact that cyber criminals are taking advantage of the main vulnerabilities of computer software. Many of such criminals are also devising different and more effective ways in hacking databases of organizations, governments, and companies. The issue is very alarming.

Participants of the regional forum ended the event by agreeing on an information sharing process to unify their actions in developing cybersecurity mechanisms. The unification takes into consideration key principles of combining and matching transnational and borderless nature of various online security threats (also called cyberthreats).

IT experts from all over the world are also warning that attempting to address challenges on regional and national levels would not be sufficient in coming up with effective and concrete solutions. The ITU forum and several other global IT organizations are encouraging global approaches to identified cybersecurity challenges.

To make cybersecurity measures work effectively, measures to enhance culture of online security through partnerships should be instituted. Working together is a key to confronting Internet threats with utmost effectiveness. Governments and online organizations should also share technical skills and appropriate investments in IT to facilitate better and wider development capacity.

On the individual Internet users level, citizens should be responsible enough in using the online media properly. They should always provide and offer help in addressing protection and security of online data. Some experts propose creation of job opportunities related to cybersecurity to further boost and enhance individuals' participation in Internet security programs.

Cybersecurity is a fight that should not be fought only by the US and other developed countries. Every country in the world should all participate to win the battle. In the future, the Internet is expected to make more things happen. It could be a better and more reliable venue for conducting businesses and basic transactions.

That is why it very important that security measures are created and firmly put up in place.

## Simple Boosts To Cyber Security

Cyber security is among the toughest issues to resolve. It has proven to be difficult since it is constantly evolving and most of our daily activities can be hit by it. How much do we rely on computers nowadays? A lot. Whether it is transportation, entertainment, communication, finance, and even daily needs. Everything seems to be computerized. What do you think would happen if these systems would crash? Catastrophe would ensue.

There are simple things that we could do to ensure the safety of our systems and computers. For your accounts and computer:

• Make sure that the passwords you are using cannot be immediately guessed. Another common mistake made is that they would be jotting their passwords. Surveys said that about 1 out of 3 workers would write their passwords. Inside attack is one of cyber security attacks, this could mean that a disgruntled employee could use other people's passwords to access the system.

There are companies, especially outsourcing companies, that strongly prohibit any kind of written password, like mentioned in the example.

• Aside from the password, there are also operating systems and applications that could protect your account and computer. Firewall for starters, should be installed and used. A firewall is a program that blocks unauthorized Internet traffic, just like how a physical firewall works. Setting up and configuring a firewall, will actually help you maximize its full potential.

Anti-virus software can be your best shot to make sure that your computer is protected, you just have to make sure that it is regularly updated. Anti-virus software would come with spyware detecting programs. There are new computers, nowadays, that are offering or already have an installed anti-virus software.

• If you have sensitive documents in your account and computer, it would be better if you would be encrypting the data. When deleting sensitive documents, then you make sure that it has been totally removed from the system. Hackers are capable of restoring or retrieving any deleted documents especially if it is not totally removed from the documents.

Electronic mails are also vulnerable to cyber security attacks. Different styles and types of e-mail scams are being developed everyday, so everybody has to be prepared and alert whenever we receive emails. Here are some signs that these e-mails are possible sources of cyber security attacks.

• The email is not addressed to you personally and aside from that the sender of the email is somebody you are not even familiar with.  Most of phishing e-mails would have an attachments along with the email.  These attachments do not even have a clear title or clear purpose.

• As your read the email, you will notice a lot of spelling and grammatical errors which indicates how unprofessional it is.

• Emails that ask you to provide financial information like credit card number, social security number, password and asking you to send some money, is totally a scam.  Banks and other institutions do not ask you these kinds of information over an email.

When you received this kind of email, do not click on any links or attachments.  These links and attachments would bring you to sites that have high risks of viruses and spyware. For example, experts would say that attachments ending in ".vbs," ".scr," ".exe," or ".pif" can have viruses.  It is best to immediately delete the email, do not even open or respond to the email.

Another assurance that even if your computer and cyber security has been attacked is by regularly saving your data and making a back-up disk.  So, if ever your computer crashes because or loses some information because of viruses, you would be prepared for it since you have a back-up.

Simple Cybersecurity Measures for Individuals

Most people in the civilized world these days use computers. The devices are not just accessories and equipment aiding academic studies. Computers are made to connect online, which in turn could facilitate actual and basic transactions. You could shop, bank, pay bills, transfer funds, reserve tickets, conduct businesses, and do just about anything you need to do online. Cybersecurity would help make you secured and safe all the time.

Because there is money across the Internet, defrauders, thieves, and burglars now focus on online crimes. Online transactions are mostly using credit card accounts, debit cards, and Internet accessible bank accounts. Thus, expect hackers and attackers to strive their best to be able to access your sensitive personal information. You might not know it but as you use your personal computer today, you might already be exposed to several Internet security problems.

How are cyber crimes committed? Usually, hackers, intruders, and attackers design and deploy computer viruses, computer programs, or software to penetrate into systems that are aimed at searching computer systems for important personal data of users without proper authorization. Viruses are rampant. They spread like wildfire and most infected computers are not identified. Thus, as you use your computer for basic online transactions, your information might also be tapped by unscrupulous cyber criminals.

Some viruses are spread through using removable hardware like discs and flash derives. Some are propagated through opening attachments in suspicious email messages. Some are most dangerous as they are automatically coming with pop up screens when you enter or open specific Websites. Downloading unsecured data online could also be a culprit. If you want to take instant cybersecurity measures, you should resolve not to get viruses from the abovementioned venues and occasions. However, you may find it difficult not to be exposed to computer virus risks.

Aside from refraining to avoid the mentioned risks, it would also do wonders if you purchase effective anti-virus programs. There are specific products that provide protection against common computer viruses. Some have protection against spread and vulnerability to malicious codes, also known as malwares. To provide you better and more options, there are many virus protection brands and products available across the market today. Their proliferation makes cybersecurity rampant and more competitive these days.

Speaking of being competitive, many anti-virus software are now made accessible to most individuals. Cost is a primary issue because not all products are affordable. The best and most effective protection is of course premium priced. If you could not afford to purchase such software, you could opt for the more affordable ones. There are even brands and products that are offered for free. All you have to do is to be patient in finding them.

You should constantly have your computer system checked. As an added protection, it would be better if you would install or activate firewall protection naturally imbedded in your system. You could also hire services of computer and IT experts to help you ensure your total online and computer protection.

Cybersecurity should never be neglected. In fact, it should be accorded with utmost importance. These days when security across the Internet is getting more serious, it is just appropriate if you would aim not to be victimized by cyber criminals and cyber threats. Cyber crimes and risks could be avoided if you know how. Explore options.

## The Future Of Cyber Security Jobs

Cyber criminals are growing phenomenally. Cyber security professionals and police, however, are in a depressing number. This is because cyber security, for the most part, is a relatively new area of information technology, recently pushed over the top by the increasing number of Internet frauds and scams, cyber thefts, system crash, and other forms of cyber attacks. The lack of focus on this area inevitably resulted in a limited number of cyber security experts. Today, there is a pressing need to create more and new cyber security jobs, which hopefully can bring leverage to the uncontrollable rise of cyber crimes.

## Growth of the industry

Now that computer and the Internet have become integral parts of transactions and execution of functions in many companies and organizations—the government included—more cyber security personnel and experts are needed to keep systems and sensitive information off the hand of cyber criminals. This means creation of more jobs, which likewise means growth of the cyber security industry.

Such jobs are necessary in both public and private sectors. Government posts are more inclined to law enforcement, military, and state protection. Jobs in the corporate world, on the other hand, are available in possibly all industries—which include business and trade, banks, and food manufacturing—to solve all kinds of cyber crimes. The growing dependence of most companies on information technology opens up more job opportunities.

## Trainings required

Schools now see the need and are beginning to offer cyber security degree programs, although most schools still identify these courses under different terms like network security and information security.

There are students who take associate's degrees and immediately take on a job, while others continue their way to university level. Still others take master's degree or doctorate. There are also those who stay in the academe to mentor future generations of cyber security experts.

Cyber security is not all about computer and nothing else. In fact, it also involves a lot of mathematics and laws. This is why cyber security professionals are also coming from other fields such as engineering and law enforcement. A cyber security practitioner, for instance, has to approach data encryption with a lot of mathematical principles. Other professionals, on the other hand, are tasked to uphold justice and take part in legal procedures, so it is necessary for them to be well acquainted with the cyber laws.

Job openings
Cyber security jobs come in different names: cyber security technical analyst, cyber security research scientist, cyber security policy analyst, among other things. In the coming years, more titles are expected to be defined and structured as the industry starts to expand. But a recent development in the cyber security industry proved that it has been having a strong foothold in the community. A few years back, the post Chief Security Officer was given a new job description. Aside from maintaining the physical properties of a company, he is also responsible for securing its electronic information and data.

The task to secure computer dependent-infrastructures and systems is a complex process, which is why rigorous training and extensive experience are necessary. Cyber security jobs combine the work of a cop, investigator, and computer scientist.

Exciting it may sound, and maybe it really is, but dedication and the will to preserve the integrity of cyber transactions should come as top motivation.

Cyber Security

The computer was originally created as a harmless aid to do complex processes. Over the years, however, the harmless machine, which is charged with almost limitless potential, has become the ground work for cyber crimes. These crimes, which affect individuals, organizations, and even governments, call for tight cyber security to cut short the possibilities of inflicting further harm. But what is cyber security exactly? And how does this protect the whole cyber community?

The proliferation of cyber crimes
In 2007, a report identified 500,000 computers as "zombies" after being hijacked by hackers. "Zombie" computers respond to the prompting of the hackers and allow them to freely break into the systems and gain access to important files and personal information through backdoors. This can inflict danger—from making unauthorized purchases through someone else's credit card to imposing threats to the national security.

There is no solid figure just how many affected computers there are now today, but reports said the numbers are higher. In fact, there was not a point of dwindling down; hacking has been projecting an upward trend. Proof to that is the unbelievably high cyber crime rate in 2008.

The current crisis in cyber insecurity puts many banks, airports, hospitals, and governments in the danger zone. It opens more opportunities to identity theft, virus dissemination, system breakdown, and other similar cyber crimes. In a much larger scale, it makes launching highly sophisticated terrorist attacks much easier.

Here comes the rescuer
To avoid such threats, computer users are advised to take cyber security measures. Cyber security is a set of techniques or guides that aim at protecting systems from any form of cyber attacks, which may creep into the system in the form of malware (virus and spyware), intruders, and hackers. Cyber security also lessens the risk of falling prey to Internet frauds, scams, and bogus transactions.

Individual users and organizations are liable to keep their computers updated, loaded with the latest security technologies, and regularly checked by a security technician. The goal here is for every computer owner to be individually responsible for his system's security. And education plays a major part. Authorities recommend every computer owner to be informed about the latest trends in cyber crimes as well as the latest security technologies to abort any threat of attacks.

There are also efforts from the government, computer companies, digital experts, and other parties to come up with a more secure, stricter, and restructured cyber environment that is regulated by enforced laws and technological systems. With the existing setup, hackers and other cyber criminals reign free in the Internet, but further security and system developments in the cyber community will allow for more fluid Internet usage and transactions with lesser risk for frauds and cyber attacks.

Globally, however, much should be done. Currently, law enforcement faces limitations in many countries for many reasons. In some instances, local concerns and issues overshadow the need for implementing efficient cyber security measures. But cyber security can't be employed by only two to three governments alone. Cyber crimes affect all nations where the Internet holds a primary place in running the government, military, economy, business, and other vital sectors. And if one nation is heavily compromised, it is not impossible for the world as a whole to become a cyber crime victim.

So, what is cyber security? It is the world's counterattack to the damaging threats of the virtual world called the Internet. And it calls everyone to action.

Unsecured: Cyber Security And Your Data

How many times have we heard about cyber security problems? Credit card information and identify stolen, viruses spreading, everybody is falling victims of cyber security crimes. The more that we depend on computers and internet, the higher possibility that we are putting ourselves at risk.

Cyber security is very much needed to be improved and reinforced, most especially since most of activities are moved by technology nowadays. Email, cellphones and instant messengers are big parts of our communications. While, technology like mp3s, mp4s, and digitized entertainment are very much in demand. Transportation would use GPS and you can even do online shopping and pay for your internet.

Cyberspace is utilized for our needs. But how safe is our information stored in computers? Cyber security's function is to prevent, detect and fight off any attacks to our systems that could put our personal and working information in jeopardy.

The risks of storing too much information in our computers are increasing over the years. These are bad news especially if your are managing your finances online, storing personal data or any work-related activities. Viruses and hacking is so common, that we should take necessary precautions to prevent it from happening to us.

According to Consumer Reports, published in 2006, there is about 1 out of 3 computer users who have fallen victims of viruses, spyware or phishing. These cyber security attacks costs consumers to spent $7.8 billion in years 2005 and 2006 for computer repairs, parts and replacements.

How do you defend yourself from these cyber security breaches? How do you protect your data? To protect your personal and work-related data, here are some easy steps that you could do.

• Use and regularly update your anti-virus software. Viruses are among the major problems, they could slow down computers, send data to other units and completely make your system unusable. If you already have an anti-virus software installed in your computer, then you would have to keep in updated.

• Spyware alert. Another huge problem is the spyware or the adware. These are computer software that could partially control or intercept your computer functions. This software is secretly installed on computer, especially if you are frequently downloading something from the internet. The good thing is that anti-virus softwares are also offering spyware detection.

• Any computer program that is being unused can be deleted or uninstalled. Too many unnecessary programs can even make your computer vulnerable to security attacks. Since you are not using them anyway, then it is better to uninstall them.

• If you are not the only person using your computer, then it would be best to separate your documents from the other users of the computer. This would prevent anybody from accessing, changing, deleting your files.  Some would have two computers, one for personal and the other one for work-related data and information.

• Use passwords, but avoid writing passwords in pieces of paper for easy reference.  When choosing passwords, choose those that are easy to remember and personalized.  If you have sensitive files, there are encryption programs that would enable to protect your data.

• When deleting documents, make sure that you have completely removed it from the system.  There are times when hackers can still restore the information.  So make sure that it is totally removed.

These cyber security measures should be taken seriously and are actually very easy to do.  These would help you protect data and information, that tool you for a long time and effort to finish.

# What is Cyber Security All About?

In this age of technology and communication convergence, you cannot help but be involved in technologies and innovations that revolve around computers, cellular phones and the World Wide Web. But as we go around our daily lives with these technologies and what not, there are times that we begin to feel really paranoid on our own safety.

May it be our physical safety or the security of our personal hardware and software. What is cyber security all about? It is in fact protecting your personal information or any kind of digital asset stored in your computer or in any digital storage device.

The first thing that you will have to understand is the kinds of threats that you could encounter in cyber space. There are different kinds of threats and each one has their own degrees of seriousness which require their own levels of solutions. The higher level the threat, the more advance or complicated the approach to implement safety measures to protect yourself from such harm.

From simple malicious codes, otherwise called as malware and spywares to serious virus that can erase the whole contents of your computer and hackers that can access and use your personal information for their own personal gain, these are the risks that you will need to address.

Oftentimes, those malicious codes or malware pass through your security system when you access a particular website or even when you open an email. These codes, exploit the loopholes in various applications and insert themselves within the computer system which enable them to replicate and infect other computers by attaching themselves to the emails that you send out or through your local network. These malicious codes are sometimes quite tricky. They claim to do something but instead they will go on a totally different path in infecting your system. These malicious codes are not isolated to malware and spyware but also refer to virus and worms which are deadlier and cause more harm.

Even though those malicious codes are quite harmful, another dangerous intruder would be hackers or attackers. No matter how you look at it, virus and worms can only do what the original programmer has intended it to do. But hackers are people and they can get the information they want and use it for their own benefit. Sometimes hackers are just testing their skills and deliberately invade your system not because they want your info for personal gain but because they are just plain curious or are just doing some mischief.

It is these kinds of things that you need to avoid that is why you have to know about cyber security and know how to handle the various threats. You will need to know how vulnerable your computers are. You have to look into your firewall and virus protection software to see if your current setup can prevent attacks from the outside.

This is why it is important to continuously update your software since new threats are being created everyday and having an updated system can help protect you from being attacked. Another precautionary measure would be to create passwords. The passwords will serve as a deterrent and help you keep your whole system protected.

With proper protection installed, you can keep your files and information safe. It is very important that you keep in mind cyber security. Cyber security is all about keeping your information safe from those who wish to access them. It is an important aspect of our lives and should never be disregarded most especially in today's computer age.

## US Intensifies Cybersecurity Initiative

The United States is the leader of all nations not for nothing. The government of President Barack Obama has announced establishment of a top-level government office in the White House to handle specific cybersecurity functions and initiatives. The announcement of the new post is apparently aimed at protecting the country's information networks and infrastructure.

The new office would be led by an appointed special advisor, to be called the Cybersecurity Coordinator. He would be part of the National Security Staff. The new office would be tasked to produce and manage national strategies for boosting, strengthening, and improving computer defenses. The proposed Cybersecurity Coordinator's office would work together with the Office of Management and Budget in keeping federal bodies maintain focus in keeping up national cybersecurity posture.

The cybersecurity czar would be vested specific powers and authorities. Aside from being an adviser to the president, the cybersecurity coordinator would also gain full backing from the Office of the President. He would have an extraordinary and guaranteed access to the president especially when there are pressing issues about Internet security challenges. If cyber attacks would transpire, the coordinator would also emerge to manage appropriate and needed government response.

The creation of the new office is expected to be a pioneer in cybersecurity practices in global countries. At present, almost all developed and developing nations are recognizing the need for concrete Internet security measures. However, governments are yet to institute organizations and agencies that would be specifically tasked to handle online security measures and issues. The US is again leading the pack. It is expected that sooner, other countries would aggressively follow suit. Many regions are also acting together to identify common cyber threats and issues. In the coming few years, more measures are expected to address pressing IT security concerns.

The Obama administration's move is expected to serve as a model for other national governments in addressing security problems across the virtual world. The US move is seen as a proof of commitment to the overall online security of national networks and individuals' (and businesses') computer systems. Among the immediate and actual priorities of the initiative are creation of national strategies, establishment of frameworks for unified responses to cyber incidents, promotion of national awareness about cybersecurity, development of strong relationships between public and private sectors, and bolstering of research and development regarding cybersecurity.

President Obama only acted on the pressing calls for heightened Internet security. In the US alone, millions of dollars are now being lost annually due to cyber crimes. Many individuals and businesses are being defrauded across the online media. The move to create a cybersecurity office is aligned with a vision to treat digital infrastructure as an important national asset. Thus, protection of IT infrastructure across the US would be a top national security priority, no less. The Cybersecurity Coordinator's Office would always ensure networks are resilient, trustworthy, and highly secured.

However, there are restrictions to US cybersecurity measures. President Obama asserted that cybersecurity pursuits of the government would not include monitoring of Internet traffic and of private sectors' networks. The government still aims to protect and preserve civil liberties and personal privacy that Americans very much cherish.

Commitment to neutrality, Mr. Obama ended, would leave online media as it should always be: free and very much open.

# USEFUL WEBSITES

Cyber Security Careers-UK
http://www.hmgcc.gov.uk/

Cyber Security Challenge-UK
https://cybersecuritychallenge.org.uk/

Cabinet Office- Cyber Security
http://www.cabinetoffice.gov.uk/content/cyber-security

Cyber Security-US
http://www.dhs.gov/cybersecurity

Cyber Security-Tips-US
http://www.us-cert.gov/cas/tips/

### ABOUT THE AUTHOR
Warren Brown is an Amazon published Author, freelance writer, journalist, copywriter, proof-reader, Law of Attraction Practitioner and Life Coach.
http://www.publishsuccess.com
http://warrenbrown.blogspot.com
Email: info@publishsuccess.com

Researched, compiled and Edited by Warren Brown.

ISBN 978-1-291-21638-7

London. United Kingdom.2012